MY
HOSPITALITY

HALLMARKS OF TRUE HOSPITALITY:
THOUGHTS & LESSONS FROM 20 INDUSTRY EXPERTS

JUSTINA OVAT

MY HOSPITALITY

WRITTEN BY

JUSTINA OVAT

justiceovat@gmail.com

ISBN: 978-978-796-277-0

Published by:

COMMUNE WRITERS INT'L
www.communewriters.com
+234 8139 260 389
6 Amusa Street, Agodo-Egbe, Lagos

Published in the Federal Republic of Nigeria

TABLE OF CONTENT

Dedication   *i*

Acknowledgement   *ii*

Foreword   *iv*

Introduction   *vi*

Chapter 1   An Unforgettable Experience   1

Chapter 2   Customer Satisfaction   10

Chapter 3   Lifestyle   20

Chapter 4   Service Culture   27

Chapter 5   The Right Strategies   35

Chapter 6   Great Hospitality   43

Chapter 7   Limitless Opportunities   51

Chapter 8   Warmth   58

Chapter 9   Relationship   64

Chapter 10   Anomaly   70

Chapter 11   A Cheerful Spirit   76

Chapter 12   Performance and Customer Experience   82

Chapter 13   Gestures and Body Language   89

Chapter 14   Love   96

Chapter 15   Good Manners   101

Chapter 16   Unconditional Love   106

Chapter 17   Kindness and Civility   113

Chapter 18   Empathy and Care   120

Chapter 19   Love as a Customer Retention Strategy   126

Chapter 20   Thoughtfulness   134

Conclusion   *141*

DEDICATION

Dedicated to the Almighty who turned water into wine.

For Sylvanus, Raymond Jnr. and Rebecca who always understand when mummy has to do her homework.

To Raymond Ovat – because only you can let me be me.

ACKNOWLEDGEMENT

The inkling to write about hospitality is one I had nursed for quite a while – indeed, shortly after it became clear that I was going to pursue a career in the industry, in 2011. The exciting discoveries I made each day while working, teaching or researching only enhanced this urge. I felt some knowledge should never be kept hidden for any reason at all.

Arriving at the decision to write was clearly the easy part. Then came the confusion about how best to structure the book to convey all that I intended to, for the audience(s) I felt could benefit from the material I sought to present. Alas, clarity came after a conversation I had with Efa Imoke (a Management Consultant and one-time President of the Calabar Chamber of Commerce who had also served as VP Hospitality and Business Develop), that went on for well over two days. Thereafter, everything seemed to fall into place.

I did need to answer one question, though: "Are you sure you know enough yet to take a position about hospitality and write about it?" The answer is what this book is about. I decided to write about hospitality from the point of view of seasoned practitioners whom I christened "Service Architects."

I e-mailed more than fifty persons but only twenty agreed to send a quote about what hospitality meant to them. And to these twenty, I say a huge thank you for believing in me.

Your definition of hospitality is going to impact the industry positively.

I have gone further, through research to expand on what your hospitality means to me. Hence, MY HOSPITALITY.

My first 20:

Amaka Amatokwu-Ndekwu, Dhiren Pawar, Jonathan Hanson, Vincenzo F. Orlandini, Chibuikem Diala, Ebele Enemchukwu, Trevor Ward, Didier Bayeye, Chidozie Uzoezie, Adedayo Adesugba, Shijil Unnikuttan, Obinna Nwachuya, Taiwo & Kehinde Oguntoye, Excel Opuaru, Geraldine Itoe, François Ojukwu-Booyse, Michael Idakwo, Brian Efa, Ntewak Umoh, Wasiu Babalola.

FOREWORD

"If you don't like someone's story, write your own"
- Chinua Achebe

It has been 25 years since I took the plunge to embrace hospitality as the lens of my professional life. Recollections of that group project challenging us to give life to our ideas set off the spark that has grown brighter each day. My hospitality is academia and the desire to develop sustainable human capital in this space. No surprise then that Justina and I met several years ago when I worked in vocational education and training at Wavecrest College of Hospitality. Also bitten by the hospitality bug, she has kept up the quest to leave an enduring legacy behind.

Who best translates experiences of hospitality into prose but those who have worked tirelessly to shape and drive this narrative of passion, hard work, and fulfillment? Who best to tell our stories than the protagonists? So, when Justina asked me to write a foreword to her book, I was intrigued. Drawing from the richness of diverse perspectives, the contributors have each brought their personal and lived experiences of hospitality to the table. Open, bare, and sometimes raw, the story is theirs and only theirs to tell. My hospitality!

But alas! Hospitality is oft-misunderstood and maligned, perceived by some as an underbelly of sorts compared to the more elite sectors of human industry. Is it a profession, a career, a job, or a passion? Hospitality! How that word evokes a multifaceted, layered, intriguing, and enigmatic reality that cries to be unpacked. It is no easy feat to explain to the uninitiated just what my hospitality is.

And now we have a book that could serve as a reference! If you are hospitality, this book offers a refreshing take that reinforces experiences of your reality. If you are contemplating hospitality, you have a sneak preview of an exciting and rewarding journey. If you are simply curious, sit back and enjoy the narrative of actors who bring rich and diverse viewpoints of hospitality to your doorstep.

Dr Belinda Nwosu FIH
Faculty, Department of Organisational Behaviour and HRM
Lagos Business School

The hospitality industry encompasses businesses involved in the provision of care, comfort, leisure, food, drinks, etc. These include businesses such as hotels, motels, fast food, restaurants, public houses, hostels, cafes, hospitals, old peoples' homes, and prisons.

The industry also expands its coverage to industrial and institutional catering services, such as consultancy, tour and travel operations. And for the first time, the hospitality industry is including the aviation and transportation industries as part of its niches.

Anyone involved in caring for others is said to be in the hospitality business. This includes housewives whose aim may not be to make financial profits but to maximise the available resources in satisfying their numerous household needs.

Isn't everyone in the hospitality industry?
— **W. A. Babalola**

As a passionate hospitality practitioner who is interested in raising quality manpower for the industry, I strongly believe that the sector's success lies largely in the hands of the employees above all else. Not just any employee, but especially those who come in close contact with guests, and are responsible for interpreting the Standard Operating Procedures (SOPs) of the establishment.

Ironically, I believe that what the hospitality industry lacks most is 'hospitality'.

I battled with this reality for ages, pondering how best to communicate it to hospitality practitioners. Eventually, I stumbled upon John Montgomery's research on the service industry. His research validated my fear - the industry is relenting in its efforts at 'true hospitality'; hospitality that enhances interaction, taking it from a mere service to an unforgettable moment.

According to Montgomery, "Hospitality exhibits itself in interaction. It could be by checking in a guest, cleaning the guest's room, taking a meal order in the restaurant, taking a beverage order in the lounge, or any other opportunity that may arise as a guest need."

See your guest as a damsel in distress and see yourself as the knight who swoops in to save the day. You must assume that your guest is new to your facility and needs your assistance to navigate seamlessly.

As people spend more money on their experiences, they consciously, and sometimes subconsciously, expect more. Guests are not only expecting tangible accommodations. They expect the intangible experiences to also be unforgettable — those services that are taken to the next level. This is hospitality. This is where a hotel's value comes from.

Example:

A guest enters the reception of a hotel and proceeds to the front desk.

Front Desk Agent: Can I help you?

Guest: I have a reservation.

Front Desk Agent: Your name? I need an ID and a credit card.

From stepping through the entrance to receiving his key, the entire process may have taken 2-3 minutes. Although the front desk agent did his job — checking in the guest — the service is incomplete and lacks the essence of true hospitality.

To emphasise this inefficiency, one can ask some pertinent questions, such as, "was there an effort at 'true hospitality'?" or "did the clerk take a minute or two to engage the guest?" The answers are obvious. If an effort at true hospitality was lacking, the hotel offered just another service, which makes no difference. We must always remember that hospitality exhibits itself in interaction.

Maya Angelou once said, "I've learned that people will forget what you say, people will forget what you did, but people will never forget how you made them feel." In what reads like a hospitality industry iteration to Maya's words here, John Montgomery writes: "What guests remember about a hotel is not just the service (the task that is expected), but the hospitality exhibited. They remember the smile and the care, those moments that made them feel like they belonged somewhere."

It is against this background that this book is written. It captures the various experiences of professionals in the hospitality space while exploring what hospitality has come to mean to them. I expect students, hospitality practitio- ners, and everyone who loves and has a keenness for the industry to benefit from this book.

1

AN UNFORGETTABLE EXPERIENCE

My hospitality is a culture where the service experience is unforgettable for both you and the consumer.
— Amaka Amatokwu-Ndekwu

Profile: Amaka Amatokwu-Ndekwu is a dedicated, America-based hospitality professional who has worked with international and indigenous hotel chains for over 10 years. She has a proven history of good leadership, tenacity, and a strong drive. She is constantly contributing to reforms, advocating for Nigeria's hospitality and tourism industry's growth and socio-economic development. Her impact has earned her several nominations and an award from the Global Leadership Institute for her work and numerous contributions.

She obtained a Management Acceleration Programme (MAP) certificate from Lagos Business School, where she majored in Business Management and Marketing. She has a certificate in Business Management from the European School of Economics, London, and a bachelor's degree in accounting from Madonna University, Okija, Nigeria. She holds an e-certification on Hotel Distribution Fundamentals from the ESSEC Business School and is a 2019 alumnus of The Castell Project Leadership Program, Atlanta.

Amaka is the Founder/President of Women in Hospitality Nigeria (WIHN). She started The Pyne Awards; the first hospitality and tourism awards in Nigeria. She is also a board member of various hospitality and tourism organisations, and a mentor with the Lagos Business School and the Cherie Blair Foundation for Women in Business, United Kingdom. She is a Tony Elumelu Foundation influencer and a partner with Interswitch Group on their payment system for hospitality and lifestyle companies.

WHAT HOSPITALITY, ACCORDING TO AMAKA, MEANS TO ME

When you hear the word hospitality, what comes to mind? Kindness? Care? The 'Good Samaritan' maybe?

I see hospitality as an unforgettable experience for both the service provider and the customer.

The culture in the way we approach situations has become a core value in various industries. From food to hotels, customers are seeking the best experience wherever they find themselves; whether on the Amalfi Coast in Italy or the busy streets of Victoria Island in Lagos. A customer's experience (good or bad) could make or mar a business.

Example:

Annabel is visiting Cancun for the first time. She is excited as she lands on the beautiful island of Mexico and is driven to her hotel. At the hotel, she finds that there is no one to assist with her luggage. 'No big deal', Annabel mutters to herself. Taking in the scenery of the beautiful hotel, she makes her way to the reception. She is treated rudely by the hotel staff, who could care less if she came from the ends of the earth to Mexico or just strolled down from her house for a quick weekend getaway. She is also left to ask for every piece of information, including the simple ones that could have been made available to her at the reception. Worse still, after booking her room, Annabel drags her suitcase up to her assigned room by herself, only to meet an unmade bed and a leaking toilet.

The hotel has made a lasting impression on Annabel. She does not think 'maybe it's just this hotel' but assumes that all hotels in Mexico are the same. The services of this hotel have left a bad taste in her mouth. Guess what Annabel will do next? She will probably leave a bad review on the hotel's website. When she is in a position to suggest exotic destinations for vacations, Cancun will probably not be on her list. Due to bad customer service, the hotel loses potential customers and, most likely, other potential Cancun tourists who could patronise their services.

Courteous treatment will make a customer a walking advertisement.
— James Cash Penney

James Cash Penny is an American businessman, famous for his numerous departmental stores around the United States. From the quote above, he believes that when a customer enjoys your service experience, you do not need to remind them to spread the gospel. They do it on their own accord.

Think about a time when you enjoyed exceptional service from a restaurant, hotel, or amusement park. Were you quick to recommend it to your family and friends?

Satisfied customers are great assets to any organisation, as no one has to pay them for advertisement. This is why organisations in the hospitality industry should spend time and resources to educate their staff on the importance of rendering exceptional services to both customers and potential customers.

Staff members are required to leave their attitudes at the door, wear a smile always, and be available to give their customers an experience of a lifetime. This is the reason hospitality practitioners have often been described as theatre artists.

AN UNFORGETTABLE EXPERIENCE FOR THE CUSTOMERS

We first listened to the customer and their expectations. Meeting those expectations means reducing friction and increasing the level of their experience.
— **Michael Levie, Partner and CEO of CitizenM**

Another way to increase the likelihood of customers having an unforgettable experience is by listening to them. How do they feel about the service you rendered to them? What do they require from you to enjoy their stay on a second visit? Would they recommend your services to someone else? When consumers feel they are listened to, it encourages them to give honest feedback, and an organisation can use this feedback to improve its service delivery.

There is a feeling of fulfilment when an organisation has a satisfied customer; they feel on top of the world, ready to conquer whatever obstacle lies ahead. As the popular saying goes, 'happy wife, happy life'. In this context, the saying would be, 'happy employees, happy customers, happy life'.

An angry customer can ruin your business. Just one bad publication from a customer can cause everything to crash. Therefore, organisations must listen to their customers and tweak their business model where necessary.

AN UNFORGETTABLE EXPERIENCE FOR THE EMPLOYEE

When employees are happy, they do their jobs to the best of their abilities. Just as employees need to make sure that customers get the best experience, organisations should also prioritise keeping their employees happy. This is possible through various means such as compensation for a job well done and a conducive work environment that gives them room to thrive.

Ironically, the employees who interface directly with customers are among the most underpaid people in the service/hospitality industry. Waiters/waitresses are paid below the minimum wage and rely on tips to fill the pay gap. This, primarily, is because there are no entry barriers into the industry. The majority of the employees are mainly unskilled and at the bottom of the food chain; therefore, they can be easily acquired as cheap labourers.

No matter how unskilled an employee is; when he is underpaid and unhappy, he brings that negative energy to work and passes it on to the customers; a typical case of 'if you pay peanuts, you get monkeys'. This is not good for business.

In as much as organisations want their customers to be happy, their employees' happiness should also be a priority. This is the second Return on Individuals (ROI); the first is caring for your customers. Ask your employees the same questions you would ask your customers: what can we do to make your stay with us a pleasant one?

However, employees should bear in mind that no organisation can meet every need. Compromises and adjustments have to be made by both parties to make the employee's experience pleasant.

CHARITY BEGINS AT HOME

If a hospitality organisation wants to create an unforgettable experience for its customers, it must begin internally. An organisation cannot build a successful business if it does not practice what it preaches. The charity has to begin at home for a hospitality business to thrive.

I know that it may be difficult for the industry to reach the point where cheap labour is not leveraged. Still, the least we can do is ensure that we develop a solid selection process to bring in people who, first, are passionate about the industry, have the right temperament, are naturally polite, and possess the right disposition to serve.

One of the minimum requirements for recruitment into the hospitality industry should be empathy. According to Brooke Cade, "In the world of hospitality, creating deep connections with your guests is important. Your hotel is their home away from home, and making sure your guests feel comfortable and welcome is a vital part of the experience. Ensuring your guests have a positive and personalised visit depends strongly on the staff and how your establishment is being operated".

Through empathy, people who work in the hospitality industry can provide better service and deeper connections with their guests. By putting yourself in your guest's shoes, you will be able to anticipate their needs, deliver your services proactively, and develop new ideas to improve the overall hospitality experience.

Beyond trade skills, we should also hire based on life skills. Providing exceptional customer service experience is multidimensional and requires a constellation of skills, of which communication (interaction) is critical. The ability of employees to communicate with empathic and supportive words contributes largely to the positive interaction between them and the customers.

Because guests are interacting with staff, face-to-face conversations are standard in the hospitality industry.
— Brooke Cade

There has been some disturbing news making the rounds about the cruise industry lately. After years of research and careful analysis, they seem to be getting a lot of bad press. A November 2019 episode of *Patriot Act* with Hasan Minhaj revealed how the multibillion-dollar industry pays little attention to its customer's needs and safety and underpays its staff who work crazy hours.

These reports made potential consumers reconsider the idea of taking their families to the sea during the holidays. Imagine the untapped market the cruise companies are missing due to bad employee/customer experience. As mentioned earlier, one bad publication can cause your business to slump.

Hospitality should be an unforgettable experience for both the employee and the customer. Hospitality starts from within. When an organisation invests in positive interactions from the inside out, it will thrive on all fronts.

2

CUSTOMER SATISFACTION

Hospitality is being able to predict and anticipate your guest's needs. If you can get that right, half the battle of making their experience truly delightful is done.
— Dhiren Pawar

Profile: Dhiren Pawar is currently the Director of Operations at Hard Rock Café and Shiro. He holds a bachelor's degree in Hotel Management. He has several years of experience in the food and beverage business.

HOW IT BEGAN

Ever since I can recall, I have been interested in the hospitality industry. This interest stemmed from my dad being an exceptional cook, with a keen sense of flavour, a nose for ingredients, and a penchant for taste, as well as the pleasure he derived from having a satisfied dinner guest. He could taste anything and replicate it. If you were not invited to my dad's parties, you were missing out! In essence, I got my love and passion for hospitality from my dad, who got immense joy from entertaining people.

I pursued a diploma in Bakery and Confectionery at Food Craft India, Pune. I then joined one of the top colleges in India, the Welcome Graduate School of Hotel Administration (WGSHA), to do my bachelor's in Hotel Management. That covered all aspects of leadership in the hospitality industry.

After a gruelling four-year course and internships, I was campus-recruited by the Ista Group of Hotels under the IHHR hospitality chain which owned, at the time, the number one spa and resort destination in the world called Ananda, situated at the Himalayan foothills in Northern India.

During my final interviews, my General Manager at the time told me he felt that my personality was more suited to food and beverage service (front of the house rather than the back). He asked me to consider changing my specialisation, which I did. I rose rapidly within the ranks, and soon, I was nominated to join their Management Trainee Programme, which would hone my skills further and prepare me to take on the role of Head of Outlet/Restaurant for food and beverage service. My training took me to various cities where the hotel was located — Bangalore, Hyderabad, and Ananda in the Himalayas.

During one of my visits to Bangalore (a city in South India, known as the IT hub of India), I attended a party at a very chic and popular restaurant, Shiro, and fell in love with the place. The next day, I had an opportunity to meet the General Manager of Shiro. Our conversation lasted about two hours, after which he offered me the position of Operations Supervisor. As time went on, I proved my mettle, and four years after, I was promoted to General Manager. Barely a year later, I took over as the Regional General Manager overseeing all three Shiro outlets in India - Bombay, Bangalore, and Delhi. During these years, Shiro won many accolades in the industry and became the most visited destination for an incomparable gastronomical and musical experience.

In 2016, the founder and owner of Shiro mentioned that we were going international with plans to open Shiro in Lagos, Nigeria. Was I up to the challenge? Some unnerving stories about Africa, especially Lagos, Nigeria, flashed by. My passion said yes, my heart said maybe! I asked if I could visit and assist in the opening of Shiro, Lagos, as well as experience the city. Before I knew it, I found myself relocating to Lagos in June 2017. It has been three years and counting. Lagos comes with its share of challenges and obstacles, but my learning curve has been steep, and my experiential acquisition tremendous, even in areas outside the food and beverage space.

WHAT HOSPITALITY, ACCORDING TO DHIREN, MEANS TO ME

Hospitality refers specifically to the relationship between a host and a guest. Hospitality is all about the guest and their experience when they visit a restaurant, about being able to predict and anticipate a guest's need. If you can get that right, half the battle in making their experience truly delightful is done.

True hospitality consists of giving the best of yourself to your guests.
— Eleanor Roosevelt

In Ancient Greece, hosts were expected to accommodate the needs of their guests. The host was responsible for caring for and providing for the guest during his or her stay. Celtic civilizations have also been known to emphasise the importance of hospitality in their culture. If a guest sought refuge in a Celtic person's home, the host was responsible for protecting the guest.

From the above, we can say that from the moment a guest steps into your establishment, a restaurant, for example, you are responsible for their wellbeing. The guest trusts that they are in for an experience of a lifetime, which should be given to them. A guest's presence in your restaurant could be for any reason: hunger, referral by a friend, or just the ambience. Whatever the case may be, it is your responsibility to cater to their every need within the boundaries of the services you offer and to ensure they have no regrets.

CUSTOMER SATISFACTION

In the real world, mistakes are bound to happen while running a business. The ability of the business owner to quickly rectify the problem is directly tied to customer satisfaction. The critical question is, what do you do for service recovery when a guest's expectations are not met?

When we speak about customer satisfaction, the oft-quoted phrase, 'the customer is always right', should be at the forefront of any organisation that wants to convert its guests to loyal customers. However, I must add that absolute customer satisfaction is difficult, especially for fledgeling businesses with limited funds, time, and energy. Every business will most definitely have that one customer who cannot be satisfied no matter the efforts put into satisfying them. I also have had my fair share of grudging customers.

I will leave you with a piece of advice from Charu Singh, Founder and Creative Head of Zooki, a platform for curated designs in women's clothing, jewellery, and accessories: "Businesses are not dependent on individual buyers; It is immature to spend all the energy to satisfy someone who does not intend to be happy. It is important to address the requirements of hundreds and thousands of other regular clients and show solidarity with the employees".

The challenges mentioned above notwithstanding, customers' complaints must be taken seriously. Brooke Cade advises that you take a moment to talk to your guests, gather feedback, and connect with them so you can gain a better understanding of their needs, preferences, and concerns. As a restaurant operator, for instance, you have to pay close attention to the demands of your consumers. If they complained that a particular meal was too spicy, the menu should have an option for the level of spice they would prefer next time. Better still, the waiter can politely ask a customer the amount of spice they would like in their meal. Make the customer feel that you are willing to prepare a custom meal to suit their taste.

It also helps to have suggestion boxes at strategic places around your establishment, so customers can anonymously drop their thoughts on how best to offer them a satisfactory experience. Swift actions should then be taken to implement such changes. Watch out for repeated complaints and tackle those first. Periodically, ask the customer throughout their dining experience if they are happy with the service provided to them. That way, the customer feels comfortable enough to open up any time dissatisfaction arises. It also makes the customer feel you are genuinely interested in providing them with the best service. This act alone could prevent a customer from leaving your business a bad review.

Example:

Ngozi calls her favourite restaurant to order some lunch. Her order is taken down, and she is told that it will be ready in 30 minutes. After waiting for 30 minutes, Ngozi decides to head to the restaurant, which is about 15 minutes drive from her office. On arrival, she is told her food is not ready, 45 minutes after placing her order. She gets upset because she is famished, and has limited time allocated to lunch.

The manager pacifies her by waiving the fee on her current order and providing her with a 15% discount on her next order. Ngozi feels relieved. Her favourite restaurant made up for their shortcomings immediately.

The restaurant can afford to waive her bill because Ngozi is a loyal customer, and tardiness is not their usual way of operation. Is Ngozi likely to recommend its services to someone else? Absolutely! In some cases, customers go on social media to appreciate the restaurant for being so generous, because, in reality, not all establishments would handle the situation that way. Because of the kind gesture, potential customers will come and patronise the restaurant.

From the example above, we have established that customer satisfaction is essential, especially if you want to thrive in the restaurant business. The trick is to under-promise and over-deliver. What do you do for service recovery when expectations are not met?

CREATING THE RIGHT ATMOSPHERE

The food and beverage business does not always begin and end with just food, although food is a critical part of it. Consumers are looking for a place to get away from all the daily stressors of life. They are looking for a spot where they can let down their hair and relax after a long day at work. Hence, the atmosphere created at a restaurant is essential. From the ambience to the setting, the music, the smell and the temperature — all these are important to the success of a restaurant business and the overall customer experience.

In her article, *Customer Satisfaction in Restaurants*, Mercedes Diaz advises that "to improve ambience, encourage your front-of-house staff to do something special for their guests. A small but pleasant act of kindness can have a more significant impact than handing out freebies".[1]

---

[1] Mercedes Diaz. 'Customer Satisfaction in Restaurants' (2019). Retrieved from https://joinposter.com/en/post/customer-satisfaction-in-restaurants

People have stopped going to certain restaurants just because their chairs were not comfortable, even though the restaurant had great food. Ignoring such a small detail can cost you a customer(s). Businesses should not focus solely on getting the meals and drinks right. They also must create the right atmosphere for their guests to enjoy and feel relaxed. Remember, you are trying to create an all-round experience for your guest; every detail should be considered.

CUSTOMER LOYALTY

In business, success is also embedded in customer loyalty. You are not only thinking about a one-off experience for your customers to enjoy, but you also want them to make you a part of their lives. Think about it. Organisations like DSTV have been able to thrive for many years because most subscribers renew their subscriptions at the end of each month. Same with Netflix, internet service providers, and websites. Those businesses are successful because they have loyal customers. The same can happen for a restaurant business; once your customers are hooked to your exceptional customer service, they will stick with you for the long haul.

As an organisation, you have to put in the work to build a loyal customer base. Providing incentives for customers and accommodating their unique needs while providing a remarkable experience whenever they visit are great ways to gain their trust and build loyalty. In the same article referenced above, Mercedes Diaz reveals that statistics have shown how every person's experience can impact the entire health of a restaurant business. The good news is that the customer's perception of a restaurant can be gauged and controlled. Study your consumer to figure out what they like, how they like it, and how best you can serve them without negatively affecting your business.

Once you can predict, anticipate, and cater to your customer's needs effectively, you have truly won them over, and that is what hospitality is about.

3
LIFESTYLE

Hospitality is the kindest way of communicating with another person while showing good gestures.
— Jonathan Hanson

Profile: Jonathan (Joe) Hanson is the convener of Hotel Expo Nigeria, West Africa's first exhibition, sales, and conference event for the hospitality community. He worked in the advertising/media industry as a broadcaster, content producer (visual/events), and marketing/brand director.

His wealth of experience in the creative space motivated him to focus on the hospitality sector, an industry he had long admired and hoped to help improve in Nigeria, having tasted what other countries are doing to raise the bar. Hanson, a Computer Science graduate of Lagos State University, aims to redefine the methods, concepts, processes, and ideas of developing the service sector beyond what is attainable today.

WHAT HOSPITALITY, ACCORDING TO JOE, MEANS TO ME

Hospitality is life. It is a way of living. It is the kindest way of communicating with another person while showing good gestures. When you think about hospitality as it pertains to a way of life, it takes what has been explained in this book to a different level. Hospitality in this chapter is depicted as a lifestyle. It is not a front you have to put up when you get to your job; it is something that guides the way you live each day. How do you treat the person next to you at the bus station? How do you react to someone who cuts you off in traffic? How do you react to a waiter who gets your order wrong? How do you speak to your spouse at home? If you want to see hospitality thrive as a way of life, you have to do a self-check.

Lending a helping hand to someone in need is an aspect of hospitality. To help others, you have to be capable; you cannot give what you do not have. If you want to be hospitable towards others, kindness has to be embedded in you first. Being kind as a service architect is not a choice; it is a must! When a flight is about to take off, the hostesses usually demonstrate some safety measures for passengers to follow if something goes wrong mid-flight. In the process of showing the passengers what to do, they always reiterate this point: make sure you put on your oxygen mask first before you help someone else. This is because a person without an oxygen mask might be in danger if an accident occurs, especially when trying to help someone else in that situation. They may be left with no strength to help themselves and many others whom they could have rescued.

Some of the most hospitable countries are the ones whose citizens are kind to each other. Such countries attract a good number of tourists each year. People want an escape from their reality, and they want to visit places that are not only rich in sights and sounds but also hospitality. How a local approaches a foreigner on the street while the latter is exploring a city or a village, and the treatment of foreigners by airport officials, hotel staff, and tour guides all make an impression. Depending on how well they play their parts, a guest/tourist will likely return or write them off forever.

Example:

Austin visited a country for the first time and loses his luggage at the airport. The airline officials were of no help, instead, they treated him rudely. Austin was frustrated. He just got off a long flight and cannot find his luggage, and no one was interested in listening to or helping him. He proceeded to the corner shop by his hotel to purchase items that he could use for the night. At the shop, he was ridiculed for his foreign accent. He headed over to his hotel room and wanted to order room service, but no one answered the phone for over 30 minutes. The next day, a gang war broke out on the same street where his hotel was located, which prevented him from going to the airport to talk to the airline about his missing luggage.

Imagine that he finally made it to the airport only to get mugged on his way back. How likely is it that Austin will recommend that country to his friends and family? What will his perception of that country be?

HOSPITALITY FUELS TOURISM

Think about the last place you visited. Were the people nice to you? If the answer is a resounding yes, then the likelihood of returning there or recommending that destination to someone else is very high. This likelihood is why places that attract many tourists are hospitable; they understand what it does for their economy. If such countries treat their tourists horribly, then their whole nation is operating at a loss because tourists not only occupy hotels and go on sightseeing sprees, but they also make purchases. They patronise the local sellers and contribute to the local economy.

Some countries generate most of their revenue from tourism. For example, the Caribbean Islands, Virgin Islands, Thailand, Seychelles, Italy, Maldives, and Cape Verde, to name a few, were quick to leverage the attention they got from foreigners. No country or city woke up and became a tourist destination just like that. It takes years of hard work and practice to create the kind of atmosphere that will attract people; hence, from the moment guests land in their country until the end of their stay, they ensure they have the time of their lives.

TOURISM BOOSTS THE ECONOMY

The small city of Waco, Texas, has seen a rise in tourism in recent years. It can boast about 100,000 tourists monthly and about 300,000 tourists during festivals. A place like the Magnolia Market at the Silos was built in 1950 due to an upsurge in tourism. The economy of Waco increased tremendously thanks to Chip and Joanna Gaines, the stars of the hit show, *Fixer Upper*. Waco became a tourist attraction through the warmth the couple displayed on their television show. The same can be said of the Obudu cattle ranch, located in my state, Cross River, a small southern state in Nigeria. It has become a tourist site for many who would rather experience Nigeria than travel abroad. This has boosted the economy of the state. Hospitality has played a major role in these places. The people realised they could leverage it to build something substantial for their economy.

In 2019 alone, travel and tourism contributed about 10.4% to the world's GDP. The industry also accounted for 334 million jobs (1 in 10 jobs around the world).[2] The economy is boosted when tourists spend money on hotels, transportation, sporting events, tours, festivals, etc.

---

[2] World Travel and Tourism Council. 'Economic Impact reports' (2019). Retrieved from https://wttc.org/Research/Economic-Impact

HOSPITALITY AS A LIFESTYLE

Most people, even business owners, only relate hospitality to hotels. They believe that only hotels and restaurants are in the business of ensuring good customer relationships, forgetting that no matter the business, a customer will only return if treated well. According to Wikipedia, "Hospitality plays a fundamental role to augment or decrease the volume of sales of an organisation; hence, every business should master it".

To imbibe hospitality as a lifestyle, you must have the following attributes:

1. **Good work ethics:** Do what is right for your guest, client or customer all the time. Give them value for their time and money, and work with little supervision.
2. **Love to deal with people:** You can only apply hospitality when you are dealing with people, so you must naturally love to be around people and love to see and make them happy.
3. **Politeness:** Being polite as a service architect is not a choice but a must.
4. **Adaptability:** Because you deal with many people with different temperaments in a constantly changing environment, you must have the ability to adapt to a variety of circumstances.

Hospitality should not be a strategy to gain more customers. Rather, it should be a lifestyle. When something becomes a way of life, it is easier to adapt to it because it has become second nature. Generally, the world is a better place when people are hospitable, and it makes those on the receiving end feel seen and appreciated. What makes life more beautiful is when people take time out to care for others genuinely.

A hospitable person, organisation, or nation is not one without people close to them. Everyone dreams of travelling to your country because the people are nice. Everyone wants to be a part of your organisation because the work culture is amazing. Everyone wants to employ your services because they would get an excellent job for what they paid for. Everyone wants to be your friend because of how hospitable you are. According to Joe Hanson, "Hospitality is at its best when people are kind to each other because everyone understands the language of kindness". The more hospitable an organisation, person, industry or nation is, the more people they attract, and people are good for business.

4

SERVICE CULTURE

*Your guests must feel welcome and pampered. You, the host,
have to anticipate any wish your guests may have. Service to
your guests must be a pleasure for you and not a duty.*
— Vincenzo F. Orlandini

Profile: Vincenzo F. Orlandini is the Managing Director of Leisure Wings and Cruise Services LTD. In 1974, Vincenzo entered the hospitality industry by working aboard international cruise ships, starting as a receptionist, and working his way up to the hotel director. After the shipboard experience, he was in charge of the leisure division of an International Group, Vlasov Group, based in the Principality of Monaco and led an international team dedicated to the management of cruise ships and hotels.

The peak of his career was establishing a luxury cruise line, Silversea Cruises, which reached the top seed of the international hospitality industry in a short time by setting an unprecedented 6-star rating (Condé Nast Travelers). Since he started his own business, he has been called to develop several leisure projects and improve the services and standards of existing hospitality premises worldwide.

WHAT HOSPITALITY, ACCORDING TO VINCENZO, MEANS TO ME

I believe it is vital to remember that service is not hospitality. Service is how you deliver a task following a job description and a standard or a minimum operating procedure; it is the process of doing something for someone. You must see service to your guest as a pleasure, not a duty. Because of the intangibility of service, your ability to create a positive, unforgettable experience is hospitality — service taken to the next level.

As the host at any establishment, you must learn how to anticipate and meet your guest's needs. Think about it this way: who is your dream guest? Beyonce, Barack and Michelle Obama, Tiwa Savage or Tony Elemelu? How would you treat your dream guest if they happen to visit your establishment? With excitement and reverence, right? Not to burst your bubble, but that is how it should be for every guest, the moment they step foot in your establishment. Do not reserve china for those you feel are of great importance.

In the hospitality industry, everyone matters; every guest should be treated as a dream guest. While they are with you, do not hesitate to ask them what they need to make their stay an unforgettable one, or make necessary changes to suit their requests. Whatever you can do within your power to make them remember you, do it. Only true passion can get you to the top. Otherwise, you cannot remain a service architect.

Hospitality is best described with the acronym below:

Home: Make your guests feel at home.

Organisation: Every single detail must be taken care of.

Smile: Always have a smiling face.

Passion: Service is a pleasure and not a duty.

Identity: Offer your guests a unique service that identifies you and your property.

Tradition: Enrich your services with local content.

Attentiveness: Anticipate guests' wishes at any time.

Lifestyle: Build a culture.

Information: Make your guests aware of all facilities and services.

Tell me: Take feedback as an opportunity to improve your service.

Yes, I can: Never use the words 'it is not possible' to answer guests. If you must say 'No' never just say 'No'; rather say 'No, but we can...'; 'No, but may we...'; 'No, but perhaps you can try our...'

H for Home: Think of your establishment as a home away from home for all your guests. Make it warm and cosy for them, even better than where they reside. Whether the guests chose your location for a quick getaway from their routine, an extended vacation, or a business trip, do not make them miss their homes. If you run a hotel, ensure the beds are comfortable, laced with plush blankets and pillows, etc. Let your guests have everything at their beck and call. Remind them that you are at their service for the time being and want to make their stay as comfortable as possible. And mean it. Don't just say the right words, show them.

O for Organisation: You must always be visitor-ready. Your guests must never catch you unawares, and your establishment must be prepared at all times to receive guests. It will be embarrassing and a total turnoff for a guest to walk into a mess instead of a well-organised environment. Your servers must be prepared at all times to meet your guest's needs in line with laid down procedures.

S for Smile: Service staff, especially those interfacing with the guests, must learn to check their attitudes at the door and put on a smile from the moment they get to work until they leave. This is why it is risky to have persons who are not passionate about their jobs handling unique customer touchpoints. Your guests want to be assured that they are welcome at your establishment, and what better way to have that assurance than by their hosts smiling and giving them a warm reception? Smiling shows the guests that you are happy to see them and you value them. Guests tend to let their guard down when they feel comfortable, which creates room for better interaction. The state of your face brings a type of energy into an environment; smiling encourages warmth and trust. Plus, you are never fully dressed without a smile.

P for Passion: Passion is what drives an establishment. If your employees are not passionate about their job, there is a high probability that the organisation will crumble. It is only a matter of time before the customer picks up on the lack of passion within the organisation. When people are passionate about their jobs, it shows in the way they care for their customers (guests in this case), and customers can feel at home, trusting that they will be well taken care of.

I for Identity: There is a lot of competition in the hospitality industry. Restaurants pop up every day, the same with hotels and other accommodation services. There must be something that differentiates your establishment from others. What would make a guest keep coming back for more? This should be the unique service that sets your establishment apart from all others in the mix.

T for Tradition: Most times, the people who employ your services are not residents where you are; hence, you must add local content to the service you provide. Let your guests know that they are in for an experience of a lifetime. If you run a restaurant, show them that your establishment offers more than just good food. They also get to experience your city, town, village, or country through the unique experiences you provide them.

A for Attentiveness: Nothing is as off-putting to a guest as a lack of attention to details they provide you with. You have to be attentive to every piece of information provided by your guest because, sometimes, if important details get mixed up, it could be life-threatening.

For instance, there was a news report about a lady who was on vacation with her friends. They went out to eat and she stated clearly, several times, that she was allergic to nuts. She could not consume anything with nuts in it, including oil. Unfortunately, she was served a meal with nuts, but the server did not inform her. She went into shock and was rushed to the hospital. She spent many months in the hospital and ended up brain-damaged and partially paralysed, amongst other things. As a result, she could not return to work, so she became dependent on her parents. And to think that her career was just beginning. That is how vital attentiveness to detail is. Your attention to detail must be impeccable as a host, so you are not slapped with a lawsuit for negligence.

L for Lifestyle: Establish a culture of hospitality and live by it. Remember, you are in the industry because of your passion for serving.

I for Information: Because of the intangibility of service, you must put out only accurate information. You must go further to ensure that you deliver on your promises. It will be wrong for a guest to arrive at your establishment, only to find out that the information you have out there is false. That could be bad for your business because they might opt for another hotel or restaurant that has proven to be accurate with their information next time. Be sure to inform your customers of what your facility has to offer. That way, they know that they have everything they need on your premises and do not have to go elsewhere. Remember, the goal is to under-promise and over-deliver - to a high standard though. Promise good enough to attract; deliver excellently to keep.

T for Tell me: If you are always polite and friendly, guests will be encouraged to share how they genuinely feel about your service. They will reveal whether or not they are happy about something in your establishment. It will also give room for improvement on your part. As mentioned in previous chapters, they would not need to go online to leave a bad review because you positioned yourself to get feedback. This allows you to solve problems promptly.

Y for Yes, I can: Your guests want to know that you can solve all their problems. Remember, they are the damsel in distress; you are their saviour. 'It is not possible' should not be a part of your vocabulary when attending to guest requests and complaints. Have a recovery plan in place; always have a solution to every problem. Find ways to accommodate their requests, and do not forget to offer an incentive; this can encourage them to come again.

Remember, your guest is your top priority when you are in the hospitality business, and you should treat them as such. If you have no passion for service, then there is no point in being in the service industry.

5

THE RIGHT STRATEGIES

Exceptional hospitality is possible only when the team believes in excellence, with an eye on the right strategy.
— **Chibuikem Diala**

Profile: Chibuikem Diala is the CEO of Sustainable Eco6tem and Founder of the International Hospitality, Tourism, and Eco-Sustainability Forum (IHTEF). He is a social entrepreneur and green evangelist with a strong interest in leadership, human capital economy, hospitality, and tourism. He has an exploratory 15-year career spanning diverse sectors, including Media/Brand Management, Hospitality, MICE, and Green Economy Communications.

Diala is the author of the phenomenal book, *Why Your Hotel Will Fail*. He is a member of the Nigeria Conservation Foundation, the Nigeria Institution of Industrialists and Corporate Administrators, the Institute of Hospitality, and the Association of Tourism and Hospitality Consultants of Nigeria (ATHCON). In 2019, he was inducted into the Top 100 Tourism Personalities in Nigeria.

WHAT HOSPITALITY, ACCORDING TO CHIBUIKEM, MEANS TO ME

Hospitality for me is all about teamwork, excellence, and the right strategies. Suppose any organisation, large or small, wants to excel in the hospitality industry, they need to have a knack for excellence and build a reputable team while developing the right strategies which would work for them. No two organisations are the same in the hospitality industry because they work tirelessly to distinguish themselves. As such, if a particular strategy works for an organisation, it does not mean it will prove effective in yours.

Hence, you have to allot a considerable amount of time to market research, which will enable you to answer questions like; What is the industry missing? How can my organisation make up for that gap? What do my customers expect from me? What measures can I put in place to make sure we are developing the right strategies to meet the industry demands without negating my customers' needs in the process? Answering these questions will enable you to streamline your services to better fit your customers' growing needs.

According to Tara Schofield, the hospitality industry offers a wide variety of services to consumers. It is a very competitive industry, so it is essential to establish and operate with management strategies. The hospitality industry encompasses all businesses related to operational and recreational services provided to consumers for their leisure. Not only does it include accommodation (hotels, motels, lodges) and food, but it also includes businesses like events management, transportation, and cruise lines.

Because there is intense competition in the hospitality industry, there is also a need for strategic management, effective planning, and processes to attain company success.

In an article published in *Hotel News Now*, the hotel guru, Robert Rauch, wrote that one popular strategy that helps companies stand out is the 'balanced scorecard'. This strategy allows a company to assess budgets and financial measurement devices as well as non-tangible assets such as customer relationships and brand awareness. In *The Strategy Focused Organization*, Robert S. Kaplan and David P. Norton state that exclusive reliance on financial measures in a management system causes businesses to do the wrong things.

Kaplan and Norton believe that there are four basic strategic themes:

1. **Build the franchise:** In the case of hoteliers, this applies to the individual franchisee as well as the brand managers. Optimise that brand name!
2. **Increase customer value:** Today's savvy customers may pay to stay in a luxury hotel, but they will require value for that money spent.
3. **Achieve operational excellence:** Satisfactory service is not good enough for today's fickle consumer; excellent service is now required. Provide unanticipated remarkable service.
4. **Be a good corporate citizen:** This comes back in increased revenues, better employees, and more repeat businesses.

The authors describe five steps necessary to create a strategy-focused corporation:

1. Translate the strategy into operational terms.
2. Align the organisation to the strategy.
3. Make strategy everyone's job.
4. Make strategy a continual process.
5. Mobilise change through executive leadership.

Example

You run a hotel that has a considerable amount of success all year round. The people who visit your establishment are mostly young adults from ages 18-29. Then you hear about a popular resort, which caters to families with young kids, and you decide to install amenities in your hotel for that demography as well.

This could work, but it would be wrong to invest so much money into the project without adequate strategic planning and hope for returns on your investments when the project kicks off. However, you might assume this to be a good move because a handful of families showed up; they could have been more. But what happens when the young adults show up and are put off by the facilities catering to kids, considering that they want a quick getaway to have fun with their friends? Families with kids may be put off by young adults, who may not be modest in their activities. Now, you stand the risk of (1) losing your potential customers and (2) losing regular customers. Success without research should not be the critical driver you use in developing your marketing strategies. You must do your due diligence first by researching before you implement changes so you do not lose your customers.

To fully develop the right strategies for your business, you must leverage these key elements:

1. **Research**: This point is of the essence. If you want to succeed in this industry, spend a considerable amount of time on research. Research enables you to find out more information about your target audience and their behaviours. It reveals where you should target and what you should not waste your

time with. As time goes on, the big picture becomes more evident to you, and you can then make the right choices.

2. **Listen to your team**: If you want excellence to be one of the critical drivers of your organisation, it has to become a collective effort. One person cannot carry the weight of the organisation alone. As a person in a position of power, you have to trust that the people on your team are professionals who know what they are doing. Let everyone brainstorm and throw out ideas they deem fit, and in the end, a decision will be made based on what is best for the organisation and its customers. If you want to excel, it will take teamwork. Teamwork makes the dream work.

3. **Survey your customers**: You need to have extensive knowledge of those who patronise your services. This will enable you to streamline your services better to meet their needs. This survey can be done by providing each guest with forms to fill out during and after their stay. The forms should include information about the guests, their unique needs, and ways you can improve your services to them. Never think that you have arrived, and there is no need for improvement. It is only a matter of time before a new establishment pops up, offers your customers what they did not know they needed, and put you out of business. You must stay ahead of the game.

4. **Location**: Location is a crucial point that organisations cannot afford to ignore. You must do your research before you pitch your tent. If not, you run the risk of getting no return on your investment. Just like social media, you have to be strategic about your location. Location matters a lot for businesses like hotels, resorts, cruise ships, and restaurants.

   For instance, in Lagos State, Nigeria, if you want to visit fancy restaurants, Victoria Island and Ikoyi are your best bet. Restaurants target that location because they know many middle-class and rich people either reside or work there. Even the local restaurants such as the 'mama put' joints are also strategically located. They know their customers: the average government worker, labourers who work at construction sites, and undergraduates. In countries like the United States, you will find various restaurants downtown because that is their business district.

5. **Have an online presence**: We now live in a time where having an online presence is as important as the blueprint of your organisation. Most customers utilise search engines such as Google or Yahoo to find what they are looking for. If your business does not have a user-friendly website, you are possibly eliminating the majority of your potential customers. It is critical that when you are building your business, you take your time to build an online presence. This applies to websites and social media.

It will help you to reach more customers and draw the right people to you.

6. **Build a customer loyalty programme**: Every customer wants to be appreciated by the businesses they patronise. If you offer them incentives through customer loyalty programmes, they will keep coming back for more, which is a win-win. You could offer them discounts on early bookings, free meals if they return, or a free one-night stay at your facility if they refer a customer. Such programmes build trust and long-lasting relationships between you and your customers.

Your organisation will be successful if you have your eyes on the right strategies. It will be meaningless to build an organisation with the wrong strategies and end up without any returns on your investment.

6

GREAT HOSPITALITY

It is in great hospitality that beautiful experiences are captured and shared even without a camera.
— Ebele Enemchukwu

Profile: Ebele Enemchukwu is a Customer Service Expert, Etiquette Facilitator, Compere, and Beauty Consultant from the prestigious London Makeup School. With a BSc, an MBA, and experience spanning fourteen years in customer service, Ebele has designed and facilitated over 600 training sessions, engaging more than 5,000 participants. Blessed with great oratory skills, excellent communication, and interpersonal skills, she possesses a powerful drive for growing others to be their best possible.

In 2015, Ebele won the Mrs Nigeria United Nations pageant. She represented Nigeria on the world stage in Kingston, Jamaica, where she won the Mrs Tourism United

Nations world title. Listed as one of the Top 100 Tourism Personalities in Nigeria, Ebele is a Tourism Ambassador and a major Influencer of Carnival Calabar. She is passionate about the revival and sustenance of the tourism industry in Nigeria.

For 4 years, Mrs Enemchukwu has worked closely with other like-minded individuals, governments, and tourism stakeholders within and outside Nigeria to give tourism the promotion and positive visibility it deserves. She has contributed to the tourism industry as a moderator, keynote speaker, TV presenter, advocate, adjudicator, event host and in many other ways. Ebele's writing prowess has seen her articles featured and shared on many online and offline platforms. In December 2019, she co-authored a book, *Carnival Calabar: A Chronicle of Themes*. Ebele is a wife, mother of three adorable children, and the CEO of WABIO.

WHAT HOSPITALITY, ACCORDING TO EBELE, MEANS TO ME

Great hospitality is comprised of beautiful experiences. A beautiful customer experience is one of the keys to building a successful organisation in the hospitality industry. Everyone is quick to whip out their phones to capture unforgettable experiences. When an experience so encapsulates a guest, they will never forget to document it. It is your responsibility as a service architect to make guests want to remember an experience by actually being in the moment. Moments need to be experienced, not photographed. Give customers an experience that will make them put their phones down.

When working to create exceptional guest experiences, do well to remember Maya Angelou's wise words. The guests should not just hear or see it; they must feel it. Remember, all your efforts can be eclipsed by poor interaction with just one staff. Therefore, you must have a strategy for delivering quality experiences, including a service recovery strategy. Companies that successfully implement a customer experience strategy achieve higher customer satisfaction rates, reduced customer churn, and increased revenue.

According to Robert Rauch, hospitality is no longer an art; it is a science, and reputation management is proof of this. Reputation management has become a strategic and integral part of our operations, sales, and marketing efforts. It is more than responding to complaints occasionally. It is about creating guest engagement, increasing credibility, and monetising the interaction.

There are millions of reviews written each day across a myriad of platforms. The web has the power to influence a person's decision-making process and managing your business's reputation will determine your success or failure. It is critical to understand the different platforms, the role they play in the decision-making process, and the tools that have been created to help us manage the feedback on review sites.

Example:

Amaka is a doctor who works crazy hours each week. Because of the overwhelming number of patients she attends to each day and the stress involved, she constantly deals with migraines, which do not subside with medications. Her husband advised her to visit a spa for a day of relaxation, to get pampered, which she obliged.

Amaka visited the spa on the day of her appointment. As soon as she alighted from her vehicle, she was greeted with so much warmth. The spa attendant had a smile plastered on her face as she took Amaka's bag. She ushered Amaka to the waiting area, which has a cool temperature and soft music playing in the background.

The attendant then asked her if she wanted tea or coffee. Amaka opted for green tea. Not only were they winning her over with their exceptional service, but their ambience and décor were also something out of a movie. When she finished her tea, she was led to a room where she would be attended to throughout her stay. Every so often, senior staff would come into the room to ascertain that their client was receiving the services she required.

Impressed by the warm reception and the exceptional service, Amaka made a mental note to make this a monthly affair.

Amaka fell asleep while they work on her body to relieve her of stress. Once they were done, they quietly stepped out and allow her some time to enjoy her sleep. She woke up from a 2-hour nap and got dressed. As a first-time guest, the spa offered her a 50% discount for her next visit if she commits to a one-year membership. She immediately obliged, looking forward to her next appointment.

The staff offered to bring her a beverage before she leaves, but she smiled and said, "No, thank you. You have done enough".

Amaka got into her car and immediately called her friend to narrate the memorable experience she just had at the spa. Her friend asked in excitement if she took pictures, and she responded, "I did not even think of my phone. I was wrapped up in the services they provided". This made her friend even more curious about visiting the place.

The spa made their client feel so relaxed that she forgot she had a mobile phone. That is what organisations should look out for when brainstorming on ways to improve their services and provide a beautiful customer experience.

A business cannot exist without its customers. This is why companies are focusing on winning new businesses and, more importantly, retaining new and existing customers. From the example above, you can see that the spa won at retaining Amaka and also gaining her friend as a potential customer.

Below are some ways through which you can improve customer experience:

1. **Treat your employees as your first customers**: If you take proper care of your employees, they will return the gesture and ensure that your customers get a beautiful experience. Listen to your employees; they are the ones who interface with your customers or potential customers the most. The easier you make their job, the quicker it will be for you to create a loyal customer base. Aim to improve your score, get your staff involved in improving the score, set small goals, and celebrate your little achievements. This will encourage better customer service from your team members and help you get better reviews online.

2. **Your customer is king**: Every organisation in the hospitality industry has to have this phrase tattooed in their minds. If you want your customer to enjoy a beautiful experience, you have to treat them like royalty from the moment they step foot in your facility until they exit it. It does not end there. You also have to follow up on them after they leave. This will make them feel valued, and people will always return to a place where they are valued.

3. **Build an emotional connection with your customers**: You can do this by asking them questions about their day and what attracted them to your service. In Amaka's case, for example, the staff can ask her what causes her headaches, and why she is stressed out, and give her tips she could use to relax at home. That way, they show that they genuinely care for their customers and not just their pockets.

4. **Manage customer expectations**: Find out what they expect from you as soon as possible. Let them know if that falls within the scope of services you provide, and if not, you will be happy to make a referral. Most scuffles between service providers and customers are from unmet expectations, but if there is clear communication from the beginning, then both parties know what they are getting into.

5. **Encourage customer engagement**: One of the ways you can improve your organisation's services is by asking your customers for feedback after they have used your services. Remember, feedback should be regarded as an opportunity to improve service. If they are happy with it, they will let you know. If they are upset, they would be happy to inform you as well. Never encourage indifference by not following up with your customers because that is where you will lose them. An organisation that is passionate about providing beautiful experiences for its

customers should encourage customer engagement to improve its modes of operation.

Reputation management is not just about responding to reviews; it is also about how hoteliers work to improve rankings on these sites. Hoteliers must implement a carefully planned strategy and have attainable goals in place.

Reputation management is the key to success in the hospitality industry. Ensure that it is a priority among your team by setting goals and being present on review sites.

7
LIMITLESS OPPORTUNITIES

Hospitality is a sector that is so varied, and so wide-ranging that it offers opportunities for everyone, whether as a customer (guest), employee, entrepreneur, supplier, or many other stakeholders.
— Trevor Ward

Profile: Trevor Ward is a specialist consultant in the hospitality, leisure, and real estate industries. He is the Managing Director of the Lagos-based W Hospitality Group and Chairman of Hotel Partners Africa. He started his consultancy career in 1983, having completed a degree in hotel management at the University of Surrey, and worked in hotel management positions in the UK. He has been based in Nigeria since 2003.

His industry experience spans over 40 years and includes advising clients on hotel, tourism, and leisure development in over 90 countries across the globe and 39 countries in Africa. With a special focus on sub-Saharan Africa, he works with many international hotel groups seeking a presence in the region and with financial institutions, investors, and entrepreneurs across the continent. He is regarded as one of the foremost experts in the hotel industry in sub-Saharan Africa. He is also engaged primarily in development consultancy, ranging from investment appraisals and operator selection to asset management, valuations, and agency.

In addition to his advisory work, Trevor is a member of the Institute of Hospitality, for which he is the Ambassador for Africa and the International Society of Hospitality Consultants. He is a founder and trustee of the Hotel Managers and Owners Association of Lagos. Trevor is a regular speaker at industry conferences and writes in various professional and Africa-focused journals, including *Africa Investor* and *BT Africa*. In 2018, he was awarded the inaugural Impact Award for his outstanding contribution to Africa at the Africa Hotel Investment Forum (AHIF), and in 2019 was recognised as Icon of the Year at The Pyne Awards.

"I have been in the hospitality industry since 1975, and it is still as exciting to me now as when I first got hooked. It is a sector that is so varied, and so wide-ranging that it offers opportunities for everyone, whether as a customer (guest), employee, entrepreneur, supplier, or many other stakeholders. More importantly, my work in Africa (since about 1990) creates jobs and therefore alleviates poverty, often in places where other economic sectors do not or cannot have the same impact. It has enabled me to make thousands of important contacts, and I have been privileged to travel to over 90 countries around the world, experiencing, advising and contributing to the growth of their national and local hospitality industries."

WHAT HOSPITALITY, ACCORDING TO TREVOR, MEANS TO ME

Hospitality is the ability of service architects to focus on quality differentiation by leveraging the value chain. The hospitality and tourism industries are critical parts of the growth and development of an economy due to the varied opportunities they provide.

According to Anjali Caldera, "Since its inception, the hospitality sector has been growing more competitive with the changing demands of tourists. Thus, tourism stakeholders should constantly monitor the value chain to understand how value can be added differently to their organisations, to attract more customers and generate more revenue. A value chain is a business model that describes the range of activities needed to create a product/service. The activities in a value chain in hospitality services could be categorised into primary activities and support activities".

These activities must be run effectively and monitored closely for a smooth flow and to retain a competitive advantage. It may be expensive to run but be assured that your customers will get value for their money. Your team will discover what strongholds to capitalise on and loopholes to close, all of which would lead to maximum efficiency and profitability.

Let us discuss this further using Michael Porter's "5 primary activities of a value chain". They are inbound logistics, operations, outbound logistics, marketing and sales, and service. Let us then apply these value chain activities to Trevor's categorisation of the value chain.

In this case, inbound logistics covers all relationships with suppliers, as it has to do with receiving, storage, and inventory control. Operations cover the conversion of policies, procedures, and programmes into service delivery. Outbound logistics covers all service touchpoints. Marketing and sales cover all strategies to enhance visibility and target appropriate customers. Services cover all activities to enhance the customer experience.

For hospitality to be sustainable, it must connect with direct and indirect tourism services to ensure the smooth flow of value chain operations.

Consider this statement:

"The National Bureau of Statistics (NBS) said the tourism sector accounted for 34 percent of GDP and about 20 percent of the nation's employment creation in 2017. Yemi Kale, Statistician-General of the Federation and Chief Executive Officer, NBS, disclosed this at the 61st United Nations World Tourism Organization Commission for Africa (UNWTO-CAF) Conference in Abuja.

The theme of the conference was 'Tourism Statistics: A Catalyst for Development'. Mr Kale said that tourism in Nigeria had immense potential and indeed, the sector encompasses and affects several sub-sectors across the nation's key output sectors. He said that Nigeria was an inspirational destination for visitors, adding that international visitors come to the country to immerse themselves in its landscapes, indigenous culture and experiences, and do business.

'This is our competitive advantage, and we need to work together to make the most of it', he said. The statistician also said that tourism activities reinforced cultural pride, the preservation of the nation's unique heritage and traditions, as well as the conservation of their environment. According to him, it is because of its far-reaching impact on all groups of society, that tourism is mentioned specifically in both the Sustainable Development Goals and the Agenda 2030.

Concerning the direct impact of tourism on GDP, some economic activities make up what we may call the tourism characteristics sectors. The art, entertainment and recreation, trade, transport, accommodation and food services, administrative, support, and other services accounted for 34 percent of the GDP in 2017 and about 20 percent of employment. Even though as you know, not all of that 34% and 20% GDP and employment contribution will be related directly to tourism activities.

Nevertheless, this shows you the immense potential of tourism activities in Nigeria, a 500-billion-dollar economy with about 70 percent of that household consumption expenditure', he added. Mr Kale said that tourism had also proved to be a much-needed source of additional income for households, particularly within rural regions."

Although this article was published in 2018, its findings still ring true; the hospitality industry is one of the country's fastest-growing industries. It has its tentacles in multiple sectors and contributes to the growth and development of the economy.

For example, destination countries such as Jamaica, Puerto Rico, Seychelles, Cape Verde, and the like have built stable economies with the help of the hospitality and tourism industry. Yearly, tourists flock to such destinations to relax, learn about diverse cultures, and enjoy experiences of a lifetime. The locals in such countries have found a means of livelihood, which can be credited to this industry. Not only that but these locals also make contact with thousands of people from all walks of life, all year round; an opportunity that can only be made possible through hospitality. That is why nations strive to make their tourism sector a well-oiled machine. Tourism indeed has tremendous effects on a nation's economy.

8
WARMTH

Welcoming with goodwill, generosity, and friendliness is the backbone of hospitality.
— **Didier Bayeye**

Profile: Didier Bayeye is the MD of Global Travel World of Experts Services. He is currently the Acting Group Manager, Sales and Marketing at Sun International for Africa and Indian Oceans. He previously held a position in Sales and Marketing as the Manager at A&K (Abercrombie & Kent) and Director of Voyageurs Du Monde Africa (one of the biggest in Europe and the biggest in France).

Didier has an MBA in Business Management, a Bachelor of Commerce (BCOM) in International Relations, a diploma in Marketing and one in Managing Tourism Industry, a certificate in Selling, and another in Negotiation Skills. He also holds a Public Relations diploma from International Hotel School and is a proud member of a plethora of associations that support and promote Africa in many ways.

WHAT HOSPITALITY, ACCORDING TO DIDIER, MEANS TO ME

We cannot speak of hospitality without mentioning the following terms and concepts:

- Generosity
- Reception
- Entertaining clients or guests, visitors or strangers

Welcoming a guest with goodwill, generosity, and friendliness is the backbone of hospitality. There is a common saying that first impressions last. The reception a person gets as soon as they step into a place is likely to affect them every time they refer to that place. While this has more to do with the attitude, appearance, and approach of the person standing as the face of the establishment, professionalism comes in handy because it helps with time management from arrival to check-in.

For instance, one of the enormous problems commonly noticed in the hospitality sector is the gap between the time bookings are made and when the guest physically checks into the hotel.

Let me explain this better. Generally, bookings are made either by phone or by sending an email. During the booking, the caller provides details about the prospective guest, such as name, email address, contact number, city or country of origin, etc. It is a good practice to fill in these details on the registration form so that upon check-in, the guest sees that the establishment is equipped with trained staff. It also reduces the check-in time because all the guest needs to do is sign the form, pay, and collect their key.

In some cases, the guest might have paid for the booking with their credit card, making it easier to identify them against any contrary document they present to the front desk. If taken into account, this process should take less than two minutes to check the guest in.

What we see in some establishments these days is that after receiving a guest's details via phone or email, upon check-in, the front staff still presents the guest with a form to fill in the same details earlier sent by email or provided over the phone. Apart from being quite annoying, such an attitude conveys a lack of professionalism and attention to detail. It is also an unnecessarily time-consuming process.

How can a hospitality establishment make the check-in process seamless and less time-consuming for a guest who shows up with no prior booking or arrangement? This could be a typical case, but it can still be very smooth and consume as little time as possible if handled professionally.

The most important step in dealing with such a situation, after the guest has agreed to the cost presented to them, is to ask for payment through cash or debit card. The second element is the proof of identity, which is critical, especially for card payments, to certify that the guest is the owner of the card. Once the proof of identity is provided, the front office makes a copy, collects payment, presents the guest with a registration form, and asks the guest to sign.

After appending their signature, the guest can then be given the room key and a brief tour of the property. It is always good to make the timing of the tour optional; see if the guest wants it before checking in or if they prefer to come back later at their convenience. Alternatively, it can be done while the guest is being accompanied to the room by the porter or guest relations personnel if the establishment has any.

This process should not take long, and the front office staff or receptionist can fill in the registration form using a copy of the guest's identity document. Should there be any information needed that is not displayed on the document, the front office may call the room or slide the form under the door for the guest to fill in the comfort of their room after checking in.

By following these protocols, the guest will be spending minimal time standing at the check-in counter, which can be quite tedious, especially when they have just arrived from a trip and want to relax as soon as possible. Hospitality establishments should give a pre-booked guest and a walk-in guest the same experience at check-in to make them feel welcome and comfortable, irrespective of how they chose to book their stay.

Providing prompt services will encourage the guest to come back for more. Guests that patronise hotels and resorts do so because they have taken time away from their busy schedules to rest or spend quality time with loved ones. Hence, it is the establishment's responsibility to make their stay as stress-free as possible by providing services that promote warmth, and relaxation, reduce stress and boost energy.

It is not your customer's job to remember you. It is your obligation and responsibility to make sure they don't have the chance to forget you.
— Patricia Fripp

Here are some ways through which you can foster warmth within your establishment:

1. **First impression matters**: You often have just one chance to impress your customers. Make sure they are greeted with warmth, maintain eye contact while speaking with them, and show them that you care by asking them how their day has been. These little, kind gestures can go a long way.

2. **Ask questions**: Your guest probably arrived at your establishment from a long trip and will be pleased if

they are informed about various amenities available to them to make their stay comfortable. Ask them what they need and be generous with the services you offer, which they might have no idea about, even if you feel it is not required in that circumstance. Nonetheless, it will be better if they know that it is available.

3. **Be friendly**: A guest patronised your organisation because they might want to get away from their hectic life. Things will be worse for them if they arrive at your establishment and do not feel welcome. Ensure that you wear a smile consistently as front office staff. That way, the guest can feel welcome as soon as they enter.

You cannot have a successful hospitality establishment if these key drivers — welcoming guests with goodwill, generosity, and friendliness — are absent.

9
RELATIONSHIP

Hospitality is often elusive, the delicate balance between humanity and human relations. It is the coming together of kindness, selflessness, and compassion.
— Chidozie Uzoezie

Profile: Chidozie Uzoezie is a freelance writer, content creator, in-flight magazine contributor, newspaper columnist, and aviation analyst. He is the CEO of The Afritraveller, a trendy travel and tourism blog, as well as the founder of the African Aviation Group.

Although a London-trained biomedical scientist, Chidozie has pitched his tent in travel and tourism where his passion lies. His works, which include numerous hotel reviews, have been published by several magazines and newspapers worldwide. Chidozie Uzoezie is a frequent traveller and has travelled to many countries both in and outside Africa. In 2019, he was listed among the Top 100 Travel and Tourism Personalities in Nigeria.

WHAT HOSPITALITY, ACCORDING TO DOZIE, MEANS TO ME

Think about the people you have relationships with and why those relationships have lasted till the time they have. Chances are that the best relationships in your life have a lot of kindness, selflessness, and compassion.

For a hospitality establishment to thrive, these three-character traits have to be intertwined.

Over time, hospitality has lost its true essence; it has been watered down to only bed and breakfast when, in fact, it is so much more. Hospitality is anticipating the needs of your guests beyond a well-arrayed room and free Wi-Fi. Although these features are important, to take things a step further, there has to be a balance between humanity and human relations, evidenced by kindness, selflessness, and compassion.

Example:

A depressed guest who has just lost his job checks into a hotel to avoid people around him who keep asking the dreaded question, 'What's next?' On arrival, he is welcomed by a team of front office staff determined to make his stay enjoyable. The personalised attention at the reception lifted his spirit.

This begs the question: what is the point of hospitality if it does not positively impact lives? If an establishment is banking only on the amenities they provide their guests with, they have failed. The most important features in a hotel are not the Jacuzzis, meeting rooms, or breathtaking views. Such features are critical when setting up a state-of-the-art facility, but a team of caring staff is what will keep your establishment running for a very long time. Nothing is more important.

When a guest feels welcomed at an establishment, they tend to let down their guard because they feel secure and at home. Trust is then built due to the value placed on the guest, which they often measure by how they are treated. Once this trust is established, a relationship is formed, which could very well last a lifetime.

A ripple effect happens when a customer is happy with your service. They are likely to do a free word-of-mouth advert for your establishment, which brings in more customers. Depending on how well you treat your new customers, they too can decide to spread the word about the exceptional services your establishment provides, which will herald an increase in revenue.

ESSENTIAL WAYS TO ENCOURAGE RELATIONSHIPS WITH GUESTS

According to an article on *Hospitality Insights*, customer loyalty programmes are great for business, but they do not necessarily encourage relationships between the hotel and its guests.

While guest loyalty programmes intended to create bonds with customers are here to stay, they are often seen as too transactional in nature whereby guests are essentially bribed with 'free' overnights and air miles, for example.

However, true loyalty is based on an emotional relationship between the hotel and the customer, not simply the result of paying people for their business with tangible rewards. Creating true loyalty goes beyond marketing gimmicks, as it must be infused in every interaction and experience that a guest has from the moment they begin to search for a room.

All interaction with a guest is, in reality, serving the customer. It includes anything from ordering a meal in the hotel's restaurant to offering advice on where to shop locally. Meanwhile, the difference between a guest perceiving a service as perfunctory or as excellent depends essentially on the attitude of the staff. Exceptional service is displayed by those who respond, not only to a request or complaint but also to empathise with the guest.

In the case of Chike, our sample guest above, he might let down some of his guards because the hotel employees received him warmly. If one of the staff takes it a step further by asking him about his day, what he does for a living and what brought him to their hotel, he will probably be comfortable enough to have a conversation with them. Depending on the level of empathy the staff shows, they would have won a returning guest in Chike.

As leaders, it is important that we set the culture of the company so that everything we do reflects putting others before ourselves. This flows from genuinely caring about those we come in contact with, and it must be at the core of what we do. There will always be issues at work, just as there are always issues in life. How we handle these issues will vary greatly based on whether or not serving others first — even our most challenging associates — is at the core of who we are and what we do. For job commitment with a purpose, we must teach character, not success. Focusing on building character, not characteristics.

To build solid relationships between a hotel and its guests, soft skills are needed. Soft skills are the skills that enable you to fit in at a workplace. They include your personality, attitude, flexibility, motivation, and manners. They differ from head knowledge in the sense that, a person (hotel staff/representative in this case) is judged by the behaviours they display in varied situations. Hospitality establishments must invest ample time in training their staff to improve their soft skills if they want to successfully foster genuine relationships with their guests.

An example of a soft skill is active listening. This refers to a pattern of listening that keeps you fully engaged with your conversation partner. It is the process of listening attentively while someone else speaks, paraphrasing and reflecting on what is said, and withholding judgment and advice till an opportune time.

Active listening is a trait that every hotel staff should possess. Without it, there is an increased chance of undermining the requests from guests and potential guests. As a staff, when you ask your guest a question, pay close attention to the details they provide, whether the question is simple, like 'how was your day?' or complex, like 'do you have any food allergies?'

The ability to actively listen and pay close attention to details is a skill that must be at the forefront of interactions with guests. It can be lifesaving in unique circumstances.

> *I have learned through my four decades in the service business that success comes down to this little triad: LOVE your customers. SERVE them unconditionally. WIN their hearts. Do this and something magical will happen.*
> — **Larry Stuart**

This quote by Larry Stuart drives home my belief that love and service foster relationships. You cannot be in a relationship with someone you do not love or cannot serve. The same principle applies to the hospitality industry. If you want your establishment to thrive, you have to be passionate about it, willing to go to war for your guests and provide them with exceptional service. That is what hospitality is all about — relationships.

10
ANOMALY

In a post-truth world, reality eludes the average human, as everything is being redefined. Hospitable people remain heavenly beings that live, work, and practice their art in an inhospitable world.
— Adedayo Adesugba

Profile: Adedayo Adesugba is a hospitality practitioner who has been in the industry for over four decades. He has worked with several hospitality management outfits and now runs a consultancy business out of Lagos, Nigeria. At one time, he was the Chairman of the UK Institute of Hospitality, the Nigerian International Branch. His passion for training has brought him collaborations with various organisations across the globe.

WHAT HOSPITALITY, ACCORDING TO DR DAYO, MEANS TO ME

Although this book is targeted at those who want to understand the industry better, it will be important to note that the term hospitality is often an anomaly in some parts of the world. Take, for instance, Adaora and her Nigerian friends who school and live in Louisiana, America. Louisiana is the southern part of the country, and it is known for its hospitality. People often greet you with a smile and ask you about your day while you walk down the street.

This is far removed from the culture Adaora and her friends grew up with in Lagos, Nigeria. On the streets of Lagos, people tend to mind their businesses, except when they need help with directions or selling. Soon enough, these young women got immersed in southern hospitality and started emulating the behaviour associated with the south.

They took a trip to New York City for an exciting time out. As they explored different parts of the city, they had radiating smiles on their faces that caught the hearts of people around them. On a train ride, a grumpy middle-aged lady said to them, 'You are all smiles. You don't seem to be from around here'.

Adaora answered, 'Yes ma'am, we are from Louisiana'.

'Aha!' the grumpy lady exclaimed. 'This must be the southern hospitality we hear about'.

BEING HOSPITABLE IN AN INHOSPITABLE WORLD

Most people are conversant with the story of the Good Samaritan, so much so that when you perform an act of kindness or hospitality, people term you a Good Samaritan. It takes an elite group of people to be hospitable in an inhospitable world because people often look out for themselves, weighing the circumstances before they step in to help, and damning any consequences of their wrong actions.

It pays to be hospitable because your hospitality can go a long way. People will always remember how you treated them, and how you made them feel.

Example 1:

Ayokunmi is in the Intensive Care Unit with his mother, who is suffering from stage 4 ovarian cancer. The doctors have given up and informed the family that it is only a matter of days before she passes away. All week, Ayokunmi refused to eat. He remained planted by his mother's bedside, hoping for a miracle.

One day, he fell asleep on a chair which has become his ally since the excruciating process began. He was forced awake by the sound his mother made as she yanked at the wires and drip lines attached to her body. Ayokunmi ran around her bed like a chicken with its head cut off, trying to calm her down.

A nurse rushed into the room and gave his mother an injection to calm her nerves. As she drifted back to sleep, the nurse turned to Ayokunmi and grabbed him, even though he was not her patient.

'Have you eaten anything today?' she asked. Ayokunmi shook his head.

'You need to eat something', she continued, as she grabs a nearby tissue to wipe the tears streaming down his face.

'You have to eat so you can be strong for her', she added, pointing to his mother. She then asks someone to get him some food from the cafeteria.

Although Ayokunmi eventually loses his mum, the act of hospitality from that kind nurse remained with him forever, although he doesn't remember her name.

Listed below are three ways you can practice hospitality.

1. **Show empathy**: Empathy goes a long way when practising hospitality. The nurse in our example put herself in Ayokunmi's shoes; she did not act that way because it was required of her. If the roles were reversed, she definitely would want someone to treat her the same way.

2. **Express care**: The hospitality industry spans many niches, hospitals being one of them. There are situations when the doctors have given up on patients, expecting them to pass away, without paying attention to their grieving family members who might require them to go the distance. While doctors know and can state if a situation is hopeful or not, they need to understand the pain the people are dealing with in such circumstances. Give them an audience and show that you still care regardless of the outcome. Show compassion.

3. **Be kind**: There is no hospitality without kindness. Everyone understands the language of kindness, even if you do not speak the same language. This attribute extends beyond the hospitality industry. It costs nothing to be kind. Instead, there is a return on investment in kindness.

Example 2:

Chidinma was going home from work one day when she encountered traffic for hours. She put her house address into Google Maps to help her find alternative routes to get home. Sure enough, Google Maps found a route she was not familiar with, but she trusted her device more than her instincts.

It was also raining cats and dogs that night. She soon realised that Google Maps had led her to a dead-end. There was a pool of water between her vehicle and the street Google Maps was asking her to turn to. Seeing no way out, she reversed and started asking people on the street for help.

Most of them advised that she would be better off going back the way she came, which was not an option for her. Then a Good Samaritan offered to lead her to an area she was familiar with. It was 11 p.m., but she allowed the stranger into her vehicle and started following his directions. She drove for about 20 minutes before she began to recognise where she was. The stranger then alighted without asking for a reward in return. When she offered to pay for his transportation back, he responded, 'I'll walk'.

She did not doubt in her heart that she had encountered an angel that night. She was thankful that the man was hospitable enough to help her, a damsel in distress.

In parts of the world where hospitality is seen as an anomaly, those who are hospitable are often seen as angels. In a progressive world, this is something everyone should practise.

11

A CHEERFUL SPIRIT

Smile is the soul of hospitality.

— **Shijil Unnikuttan**

Profile: Shijil Unnikuttan is a passionate hotelier with 16 years of industrial experience. He holds a master's and a bachelor's degree in Hotel Management and an MBA in Finance Management. Shijil began his career as a chef and was a successful executive chef at a couple of branded hotels for close to 10 years before becoming a General Manager.

WHAT HOSPITALITY, ACCORDING TO SHIJIL, MEANS TO ME

It is impossible to discuss hospitality without addressing the need for a smile and cheerfulness. A cheerful spirit is an essential attribute everyone in the hospitality industry must possess to remain in business. How you welcome your guests on their arrival at your hotel can make or mar the future relationship between you and that guest. As they say, 'The first impression matters a lot'.

For a guest who has had a bad day, a warm, cheerful welcome radiates an energy that can ease his pain or make his day a bit better.

Example:

Have you ever visited a restaurant and while you were there, the staff staged a birthday surprise for a guest and presented him with a courtesy cake? The guest would be all smiles, and the staff as well because they just made him feel special. This sort of treatment could encourage patronage and boost revenue for the organisation because people will always return to a place where they feel welcomed.

Although this culture of warm welcome happens more outside Nigeria, some restaurants in the country are making adjustments to imbibe it in their operations because of its positive impact on the customer and the organisation.

If organisations want to foster and maintain a cheerful spirit in front of clients, it has to begin from within. You cannot dish out what you do not have. If the culture within an organisation is toxic, it is only a matter of time before that toxicity begins to slip through the cracks. Those in management positions in hospitality organisations must encourage cheerfulness internally by treating their employees fairly so they can also be pleasant towards guests. For cheerfulness to be fostered effectively, it has to be a collaborative effort.

Here is the Business Dictionary's definition of teamwork and its effects within a hospitality organisation: 'The process of working collaboratively with a group of people, to achieve a goal. Teamwork is often a crucial part of a business, as it is often necessary for colleagues to work well together, trying their best in any circumstance. Teamwork means that people will try to corporate, using their skills and providing constructive feedback, despite any personal conflict between individuals'.

Everyone in an organisation, from the CEO to the least employee, has to be a team player regardless of the mood they leave their homes with each day. Such attitudes should be checked at the entrance of the organisation. A cheerful culture within an organisation encourages employees to genuinely care for each other. If an employee shows up to work in a foul mood, it is the responsibility of his colleagues to find out what the problem is and also find means to cheer him up. A CEO or manager who is always grumpy cannot hold an employee accountable for not being cheerful or wearing a smile.

Smiling as an outward expression of cheerfulness is a necessity and not an option in the hospitality industry. When a work environment is void of toxicity and drama, and everyone genuinely cares for each other, the employees will extend such joy to the customers. On the contrary, if the employees are having a hard time within the organisation, and there is an enormous amount of disarray going on, the customers will pick up on that energy, which is bad for business.

*— **German Castano***

"Smiling is as much a reflection of an organization as it is a validation of that organization's promise. It helps form the customer's first impression, an indication of a pledge to offer a satisfactory product or service. It plays a role in everything we do, in every transaction we touch, and in our relationship with every customer. It starts before we first interact with our customers, and it certainly does not end when the transaction is complete.

Smiling tells our story beyond first impressions. It is a personal touch that extends our customer service promise and reflects our passion. Smiling says that we want to be here serving our clients and customers. It says that we are ready and willing to go the extra mile. And we smile even when we are not face-to-face with clients or customers. Our tone of voice on the phone and the style of our correspondence communicate a virtual smile — or the lack thereof.

We cannot control everything that unfolds during customer interactions, but we always control the attitude we convey, such as amiability, energy and excitement, as well as a commitment to satisfying the customer's wants or needs. Even though a smile can't solve every problem, in many cases, our attitude can triumph over many complications that can occur during the transaction and our smile can become a competitive edge".[3]

THREE EFFECTIVE WAYS TO PROMOTE A CHEERFUL SPIRIT WITHIN AN ORGANISATION

1. Employee training: At this point, training might begin to sound like a broken record, but it is a critical part of the industry that organisations cannot afford to overlook. When an organisation takes the time to train its employees, it boosts the employees' confidence and communicates to them that they are valued. It also increases the organisation's revenue when the knowledge gained is applied.

2. Team bonding experiences: Most times, employers expect their employees to forge a bond without creating the appropriate environment for them to do so. Team

---

[3] Kaan Turnali. '4 Reasons Why Excellent Customer Service Should Start With A Smile' (2017). Retrieved from https://itpeernetwork.intel.com/4-reasons-excellent-customer-service-start-with-smile/#gs.2uclqp

bonding experiences allow employees to build relationships in a more relaxed environment. Team bonding fosters trust between employees and encourages them to be open and pleasant towards each other. That way, they work seamlessly with each other, which breeds a cheerful workplace culture.

3. A safe work environment: An employee tends to be more cheerful if he feels safe within the organisation. Every employee wants to know that their employer/organisation values them. It makes them feel safe, knowing that their jobs are not threatened, and if they have any issues with anyone, they can be resolved amicably.

A thriving organisation is one where cheerfulness and smiling have become part of its assets. Customers want to feel welcomed from the moment they visit your establishment until they leave. Ensure that you make it an unforgettable experience for them.

12
PERFORMANCE AND CUSTOMER EXPERIENCE

Hospitality is the reception and interaction with guests or strangers with warmth, friendliness and generosity as if financial rewards and reviews didn't matter.
— Obinna Nwachuya

Profile: Obinna Nwachuya is in the business of helping inspired corporate and leisure clients create exceptional travel and event experiences worldwide. As Principal of Sluxia, a full-service travel and event agency, he leads a team of professionals behind some of the most interesting conferences, festivals, and business events across Africa and Europe.

WHAT HOSPITALITY, ACCORDING TO OBINNA, MEANS TO ME

The main aim of every business is to meet the expectations and needs of their guests, which is why organisations keep improving their services. But while upgrading their services, some organisations often ignore the emotional needs of their guests.

I believe that hospitality goes beyond the four walls of the hotel, which is evident in how various hospitality companies operate. We must understand that the emotional needs of clients are as important as their physical needs, and as such, must be treated as paramount. If you must run a hospitality organisation, then you must have a grip on emotional intelligence.

It is not enough to offer good services. In his book, *Good to Great*, Jim Collins wrote that a transition from offering just another (good) service to offering top quality requires a deliberate leap into greatness. This can be quite difficult because most people are satisfied with the good service they offer, which clouds their ability to take that leap, but a deliberate change in your operations will propel you to make the impact you want to attain.

Example:

Fredrick has just moved into town and decides to check out an event centre he saw on his way into town. He got to the event centre and approached the receptionist, but her attention was on her phone. Feeling ignored, he stood for a few seconds, smiled, cleared his throat and greeted the receptionist to make his presence known.

She looked up and said, 'Hello, how may I help you?'

'Well, I just got into town and was wondering if I...'

While speaking, Fredrick noticed an unconcerned look on her face. He decided to skip the introduction and ask about the services they offer.

She responded, 'What exactly do you want? Is it a grand event or a small gathering?'

He was a bit confused because he wanted an elaborate description of their services to be sure it is the perfect location for his company's get-together.

The receptionist, as the first point of contact and the chief pioneer of hospitality, has failed to meet the demand for customer experience. This will not go down well as the organisation is about to lose a prospective client, who, at the first point, should have been treated as a welcomed guest.

If the receptionist had given the guest a listening ear and opened up for a conversation, he would have talked more about his hospitality need, but she missed that opportunity. She could have informed him about their services and probably shown him around the facility to give him a feel of what they do, but her lack of performance skills cost the company a prospective client. If only she knew his appearance was not a reflection of his true identity and its benefits to her company!

The host, be it the management, receptionist or any staff member of an organisation, is charged with the responsibility of hitting a soft spot in the hearts of their guests. Failure to do so is detrimental to the growth of the company. Why? Every guest warmly welcomed is a prospective repeat client, but they may just be another one-time guest in the absence of a good host performance strategy.

The host who interacts with clients is meant to radiate love, warmth, peace, generosity, and friendliness. Even outside the workplace, the impression you leave can either bring to you or take from you the opportunity to increase your clientele. You must understand that everyone you come in contact with could be a prospective client or a link to your prospective client.

I believe that strangers and guests must be treated with love, generosity, friendliness and warmth to satisfy their emotional needs. The point on the need for performance and customer experience in every organisation is best explained in the table below, which differentiates between service and customer experience (hospitality).

Differences between Service and Hospitality[4]

Concepts	Hospitality	Service
Who is it for?	Guests	Customers
What is the economic display?	Generosity	Parsimony
What is the delivery goal?	Performance	Customer service
What are the security concerns?	Guests or Strangers	Goods and processes
What are the factors of demand?	Sensations	Benefits
What are you offering?	Memorable	Intangible
What is the timing?	Lots of little surprises	Delivered on demand

---

[4] Nigel Hemmington. 'From Service to Experience: Understanding and Defining the Hospitality Business' published in *The Service Industries Journal*, September 2007, Volume 27, Number 6. Retrieved from https://core.ac.uk/download/pdf/76889.pdf

The table above shows the different strategies for organisations that value hospitality and those that value the show of their services. From the table, we can see that being hospitable is guest-inclined and treats the guest as more than just another customer.

Economically, a service-driven organisation spends less time satisfying their clients even though they aim to keep them. But an experience-driven company would spend more time satisfying their guests' needs, including the unspoken ones because they understand that in the end, generosity puts smiles on the guests' faces. This, in turn, makes them the guests' favourite, and more revenue is generated through recurring visits, great reviews and honest feedback which improves the company's performance.

Hospitality is upholding a standard company performance mixed with true customer experience to satisfy the guest. Your manner of approach to all your guests, irrespective of their class, should always be standard, and your desire to please them or tweak a service in their favour is the generosity you bring to the table.

Service without hospitality is just another transaction.
Forget the competition, it is not about the best company but
about being the guests' favourite.
— Danny Meyer

Danny Meyer, the founder and Chief Executive Officer of Union Square Hospitality Group (USHG), also acknowledges that hospitality is a great business strategy. He points out that service and hospitality are different. Hospitality involves dialogue between guests and hosts (staff), and customised service is true proof of its essence. The skills necessary for a memorable customer experience include emotional intelligence, integrity, work ethic, self-awareness, kindness, generosity, and intelligence.

These qualities are determinants and qualifiers for an experience-driven company hiring an employee. They should ensure top performance and quality customer experience.

Inevitably, the most useful qualities have nothing to do with IQ, grades, or family connections. You're looking for three things, generally, in a person: intelligence, energy, and integrity. And if they don't have the last one, don't even bother with the first two.
— Warren Buffett

Buffett further says that integrity is a characteristic one must inculcate, and it cannot be taught in school or learnt. It is a choice that only you can make.

As I pull the plug on this, I leave you with this self-defining question: aside from the top expensive services your company offers, what else can your client boast to have gained from your company?

13
GESTURES AND BODY LANGUAGE

Hospitality is the courteous demonstration of holistic gestures to guests with a sense of satisfactory service delivery in a well-relaxed homely and hospitable manner with great courtesy.
— **Taiwo and Kehinde Oguntoye**

Profile: Taiwo and Kehinde Oguntoye are the co-founders of Twins World Creations (TWC), an organisation established a decade ago to research and develop the relevance of twinning to the tourism sector of the world's economy. TWC has developed products on twinning, among which is the Nigeria Twins Festival, which has metamorphosed into a world-class festival and is set to host the world's largest gathering of twins.

Taiwo and Kehinde are professionally trained in the tourism business with graduate diplomas in Travel and Tourism Management from the Institute of Business Technology Management of Nigeria. They are associate members of the professional body.

The duo have attended travel, tourism, and hospitality events at local and international levels, and also travelled across Africa, Asia, and America to promote twin tourism.

WHAT HOSPITALITY, ACCORDING TO TAIWO AND KEHINDE, MEANS TO ME

Hospitality is admitting your guests with warmth and openness. It is about doing everything to ensure the guest's heart feels more than just the services rendered but also appreciates the memories created.

Hospitality involves verbal and non-verbal communication such as smiles, nods, gestures, and eye contact, which create room for proper assimilation of directions and responses. If the wrong signal or impression is sent out, it could tarnish the company's image, which is why the proper knowledge of gestures and body language is needed to ensure that the right message is passed across.

Example 1:

Ulomma had just gotten out of a heated conversation at work. Stressed, she decided to stop by a restaurant for dinner before heading home. At the restaurant, the security

Incidences, like the one above, are why there is a need for uniformity among staff regarding services and how guests should be treated. Ulomma's reception at the restaurant entrance was heart-warming, but on getting to the counter, it became a different story. She did not get the feeling that she was expected and welcomed, and it rubbed off negatively.

If only the counter staff knew more about emotional labour, she would have matched her expression to meet the workplace goals. Emotional labour is managing your feelings and gestures to fulfil the emotional requirement of a job, suit an environment, or meet workplace goals. The truth is, we cannot always feel happy or excited, but we must learn the art of showing pleasant non-verbal expressions. Irrespective of the situation you are faced with, putting up the right expressions is paramount if you must keep that guest or customer.

Emotional labour can be characterised by surface acting and deep acting. The former is response based. That is, you do not feel emotions, but you just need to put up an expression to meet the workplace demands. The latter, as the name implies, involves getting deep into the act so that you do not just express the emotion but feel it.

Hospitality should involve the proper use of body language and gestures that portray the reception you aim to pass across to your guests. In a Ted Talk, Allan Pease defined body language as varying outward expressions of your emotions that should be used carefully to avoid passing across the wrong message. The kind of body language you put up will make the guest either believe or doubt your competence.

Example 2:

Mary narrated how amazed she was when, on getting to a hotel's restaurant, she was immediately approached by a lady, Rita, who took time to inquire about her pleasantly. She said Rita used the right emotions, facial expressions, and body language to give her a soothing welcome, which made her comfortable.

Hospitality in service companies is important and involves obscuring some of our emotions. It is evident in the service personnel at some workplaces, including the bouncer at an event who has to look and act tough, and the waiter who has to look unperturbed by the unfiltered attitude of guests.

With our exposure to tourism and visits to diverse parts of the world, we have grown a defining perspective on hospitality, which relates to non-verbal communication to offering warm and homely services. Hospitality is enhanced when the beauty of gestures is integrated. Gestures are a great way to connect with your guests; however, you also need an in-depth knowledge of body language and how to maximise it. It is also imperative that you understand how to read body language as this will better direct your gestures and response to clients based on their mood.

Imagine visiting a store after a heated conversation with your boss. The last thing you want is someone wasting your time with unnecessary conversation, right? Then again, there are some gestures you'd find soothing and pleasant even in tough times, which are much better than long talks. It could be a smile alongside a simple hand gesture or even body language.

Good service, well-delivered service, is achieved when a customer's expectation is met. The problem is, we are past the age of good service. We have moved into the era of great or exceptional service. Hospitality is making your good service memorable. Once this is achieved, you have delivered an excellent service.

Imagine walking into a dark room and turning on the lights. Following that action, you can say that your expectations have been met, which is a good service. But if the light doesn't come on, it can be classified as poor service. What if the lights come on, you turn on the TV and are accompanied by a display like, 'Welcome to this room'? That is something memorable, right? It is not the norm, so it can be termed excellent service.

On the other hand, imagine there is a mix-up in the warehouse of a clothing store, and the wrong colour of items was accidentally handed over to three customers.

Suppose the unsatisfied and disappointed customers confront the customer service rep, who responds, 'Oh, I'm sorry to hear that. I am going to do an exchange right now and get you the item you ordered'.

After checking the warehouse, the customer service rep returns to meet the customers. 'So sorry, but we don't have that colour anymore. Can I make an exchange with another colour you may be interested in?'

Customer 1: 'You don't have that colour? I was supposed to use this as a gift tonight'.

Customer 2: 'Well, an exchange would be great. Thank you for your help'.

Customer 3: 'No, this is awesome. I like it. I am keeping this one'.

Understanding that each customer is entitled to his perspective, what do you think is each customer's review of the services rendered?

The first customer must have felt he received poor service because the company did not meet his expectation and he could not give the gift out that night as expected.

The second customer did not think the service was poor because the issue was resolved after the mix-up.

The third customer felt he received excellent service. He loved the new colour, and the customer rep's response and gestures made him feel it was more than an ordinary service.

Sometimes, it is the little things that make the difference. Some people are okay with just the little things, while others are not satisfied even with the sight of exceptions. In the end, all that matters is how best we understand our guests and the mark of exceptionality we leave on each of them, whether we are appreciated or not.

14
LOVE

Hospitality is a way of life. Hospitality is life.

— Excel Opuaru

Profile: Excel Opuaru has, over the years, built an excellent hotel management career while showcasing vanguard experience in the hospitality industry since 2004. He is currently the Managing Director for XcellenciO Hospitality.

WHAT HOSPITALITY, ACCORDING TO EXCEL, MEANS TO ME

Hospitality is showing love and care without restriction in daily activities. It is a lifestyle where everyone appreciates one another without holding back, irrespective of race, background, ethnicity, language, etc. Hospitality is a courtesy to humanity, and an act of hospitality is enough to melt a stony heart.

Hospitality is a display of selfless love that directly impacts the recipient, even beyond our expectations. Genuine hospitality is providing guests and strangers with a peaceful, secure, and homely environment without judgment. It is where the cure to distress and depression lies.

In an environment rife with recruitment difficulties, employee burnout, and high turnover, there is just one place to start — hospitality!

Hospitality has evolved from being an industry into a unique strategy that guides and boosts growth. It is now a practice that enhances living and relationships. Most organisations fail to recognise the essence of hospitality as a virtue that must be present among employees. This is because an act not exhibited by the employers will eventually be found lacking among the employees.

It is difficult to emulate and constantly uphold an attitude not expressed in an environment, be it in the workplace or at home. The heads or leaders of organisations have a role to play in imbibing this lifestyle into their employees consciously or unconsciously.

Make hospitality the lifeblood of your business. Let it run freely through every vein, from the CEO and senior executives to managers, and staff. This way, it flows easily to the guests and keeps them returning for more good experiences. Hospitality, without mincing words, is the defining factor of life. It defines how we treat people and even ourselves.

Jacco Van Teeffelen, hotel manager of the Fairmont San Francisco (United States), once said in an interview that hospitality is not a job but a way of life that must be taken seriously. It transcends the hospitality industry into our individual lives to help us accommodate the world's diversity. When you understand this, you begin to see the beauty in the world's diversity.

Focus on living a hospitable life, not just at your workplace but everywhere you find yourself. When interacting with strangers within or outside your office, you should show that their words matter and that they have your attention. Sometimes, we communicate this mostly to only our loved ones, which is wrong. The hospitality mindset makes us hospitable in every interaction or connection we make because we understand that it is a way of life.

Those who lead hospitable lives find joy and meaning in this type of interconnectedness. It is a way of life that transcends boundaries, cultivating compassion, trust, and community.

Example:

Richard left the office in haste because his pregnant wife had called him to get her a delicacy she was craving. On his way, a driver who was also in a rush bumped into his car. Furious, he got out of his vehicle and discovered that it was only a scratch. He looked at the other driver and said, 'You should be more careful next time. It could have been worse'.

Richard could have been aggressive and uncivil, but he was not. Looking at the other driver furiously showed that he was angry, but the level of the hospitality lifestyle he had imbibed brought back his civility.

People who lack hospitality would have reacted rudely because of the pressure from the thought of meeting up with his wife's demand. This is a major reason people engage in unnecessary quarrels; a situation that could have been easily resolved is blown out of proportion with many emotions killed and civility thrown into the gutter.

Hospitality can range from affection to meeting needs, understanding people and situations, and providing solutions. It is amazing how this selfless lifestyle improves the relationship between different outsiders.

Hospitality as an attitude is seen when a person displays an unconditional show of care and love. Dusit Hospitality Management College gives a few hints about what true hospitality entails.[5]

1. Give gifts to show how you care: Who doesn't appreciate it when they receive gifts? When someone comes to your home and gives you a gift, that's going the extra mile. Giving a thoughtful and meaningful gift shows that you value your guests and want them in your

---

[5] Dusit Hospitality Management College. 'Best Examples of Hospitality' (2020). Retrieved from https://dusitcollege.ph/beyond-education/news-and-events/best-examples-of-hospitality

company. It is also not about getting expensive gifts. It is the idea that you spent effort not just buying a gift but also thinking of one that will suit them, and one they will love.

2. Extend your help: Another way of showing hospitality is by giving help whenever you can. Maybe you can help move furniture or clean the front of their house. Be it a minor or major one, a little help can go a long way. Helping out a friend or a neighbour displays how much you love and care for them. It can also be a great way to bond with someone.

There is so much that a neighbour may be willing to share if he knows he is not alone. Often, however, we are too engrossed with what we want that we forget to lend a helping hand to the people around us. This is selfish, and it doesn't depict the hospitality lifestyle.

Hospitality can be likened to servanthood — being selfless without compulsion and setting the needs of others over yours. Although many people have described hospitality from diverse perspectives, every perspective sees love and care as being fundamental to it. It is people-oriented and not dependent on circumstance because good manners should be constant and capable of withstanding the waves of incivility.

15

GOOD MANNERS

Hospitality is an exhibition of love and care done professionally. It is what our parents referred to as 'good manners'. If we imbibe and practice hospitality as a lifestyle, only then will professional practice that is customer-focused become seamless.
— **Geraldine Itoe, GCPE**

Profile: Geraldine Itoe is a seasoned tourism expert with over ten years of professional experience in MICE (Meetings, Incentives, Conferences, and Events) and destination management. She is the CEO of NovaRosta Ltd, a travel and destination management company that provides professional planning solutions and consultancy to individuals, groups, and corporations who book MICE, holidays, corporate or group travel, and special visitor programmes across the world.

She is an IATA-certified professional in Travel and Tourism and holds a bachelor's degree in History and

International Studies from the University of Calabar, Nigeria, a master's certificate and a GCPE (Global Certification in Professional Events) from the International Institute of Event Management in California, USA.

Geraldine began her tourism career in 2008 at the Tinapa Business and Leisure Resort, Calabar. There, she managed several conferences and event groups, ranging from small meeting groups of ten participants to over ten thousand delegates (recorded as her highest-attended conference planned in 2012).

She advances her clients' mission with a great deal of experience by maximising the best of both worlds on every business, leisure travel, or event experience with the most cost-efficient approach. She is one of Nigeria's Top 100 Tourism Personality for the year 2019. Her positive energy, upbeat personality and winning attitude, along with years of field experience and industry knowledge, make her the go-to business and leisure travel, and destination partner.

WHAT HOSPITALITY, ACCORDING TO GERALDINE, MEANS TO ME

Hospitality means being selfless. Whether you are familiar with them or not, the ability to accommodate others is proof of good manners. Having good manners gives you an edge in life and the hospitality industry. In like manner, having skills in the industry is great but having a positive attitude solidifies it.

Attitude is cultivated from thought. The way we relate to situations and people around us, and our disposition towards them is a reflection of our thoughts. A person with a positive attitude or personality easily adapts to things compared to one with a traditional personality. A positive attitude can help us to stay calm in chaotic situations.

Having reputable manners earns us the respect and love of others. Equally, it helps us to better understand how they feel and leave a good impression. Reputable manners include empathy, friendliness, positivity, sympathy, and understanding.

Leaving a good impression should be our priority wherever we find ourselves. Leaving a good impression on people makes them feel valued and also makes you feel good. We can leave a good impression on others by meeting their physical or emotional needs, either directly or indirectly.

If you have good manners, there will be a sense of responsibility to others. You will always love to create a hospitable atmosphere where people can relate in a relaxed manner and be their true selves. Having good manners leads to outstanding success in our jobs and other activities.

A positive disposition develops our mindset and helps us to see the best of things and be happy. We should choose our circle wisely and stay away from negativity. Being intentional about the kind of people we bring into our space or devote our time to will relieve us of stress. Just as being positive is infectious, being negative can also be infectious, so we must be intentional when choosing our circle of friends. Individually, it is advisable to pattern a barricade against negativity in our minds and around us. Examples of such negativity are complaining and gossiping.

You can create a positive disposition by engaging in positive reasoning, nursing productive thoughts, and cultivating a habit of gratitude towards life and people. This kind of atmosphere stirs an energetic and happy feeling that illuminates our lives and the people around us. A positive attitude is infectious; it keeps bad energy off.

HOSPITALITY IN THE WORKPLACE

We should be hospitable to our clients by meeting their requests. By doing this, we are creating memories that would paint a better future or collaboration with them. We need to create a positive environment in our workplace because it impacts our level of success and that of our team members. An environment that is free of hostility makes workers operate at their best capacities without holding back.

To be a hospitable person in the workplace, you must first be hospitable to yourself. We can only give out what we have. It is when we are a better version of ourselves that we can help others. When we are happy, we can make others happy, too.

Creating a hospitable environment at our places of work helps us to make better decisions, achieve our goals, and stay focused. Being hospitable includes smiling, offering friendly gestures, taking out time for others, standing in for our co-workers when necessary, and not being pretentious. It fosters good relationships among workers and also allows people to view you in a favourable light.

A hospitable workplace encourages growth because when employees feel valued and loved, they are motivated and more committed to achieving the company's goals. They also become more productive and communicate better amongst themselves. A positive environment establishes a work-friendly atmosphere and energy. Having a positive attitude can be a gateway to greater achievements in our careers.

16

UNCONDITIONAL LOVE

Essentially, hospitality welcome(s) a group of people and ensures that they are well taken care of.
— **François Ojukwu-Booyse**

Profile: François Ojukwu-Booyse is a strategic-thinking individual with expertise in turning low-performing organisations into top revenue producers and improving customer relationships. He is enthusiastic about applying his vast knowledge to dynamic challenges while wearing many hats to promote growth and operational improvements.

He has extensive knowledge in four and five-star hospitality: hotel and lodging, catering, and restaurant management experience along with international, remote and hostile camp management experience. His experiences include all departments and sectors of the hotel, lodge, camp, restaurant, catering operations, and administration.

In 2010, as part of the Cross River State Government's drive to standardise and develop hospitality and tourism in the state, Francois was inaugurated as Head of Standards, Licensing and Quality Assurance at the Cross River State Tourism Bureau. He was mandated to compile and implement industry regulations, quality and service delivery standards, and grading systems.

He has a collective experience of 27 years in the local and international hospitality industry at different levels, such as front office, back office, administration and finance, room divisions, housekeeping and laundry, food and beverage, restaurant, facility and maintenance, guiding and hunting, game management and hotel, lodge, and camp construction.

WHAT HOSPITALITY, ACCORDING TO FRANÇOIS, MEANS TO ME

The word hospital comes from the Latin word 'hospes', meaning guest or host. From 'hospes' comes the Latin word 'hospitalia', which means an apartment for strangers or guests. This shows that, essentially, hospitality is to welcome all kinds of people and ensure that they are well taken care of.

Strangers or people we know from a distance are entitled to the same love and care we show to our loved ones. But true hospitality is gradually becoming extinct because the world is becoming selfish, and hospitality is now expressed with ulterior motives. When we feel there is nothing more to be gained from people, they begin to irritate us, and the hospitality we once showed them begins to diminish until there is nothing left.

Being hospitable is not always easy. It requires patience, love, care, generosity, friendliness, good social skills, and many more qualities. Hospitality can only be achieved if the management of hotels, restaurants, and other hospitality enterprises possesses the above-mentioned characteristics and express them to everyone they come in contact with, including staff, strangers, and guests. When these characteristics are properly implemented, it attracts visitors and enthrals new guests.

Chris Nassetta, the Chief Executive Officer of Hilton, a top-notch customer-experience-driven hotel, shared his view on hospitality and the major tactics in delivering excellently. He made it clear that his team is as important as the guests; so, the management never stops thinking of how best to make their jobs easier, faster, and better. He also added that Hilton is a family, and all team members are treated as family. He said, "If we treat them like family, guess how they're gonna treat you as a customer when you walk through the doors. While you're with us, you become part of our family".[6]

---

[6] Great Place to Work. For All Leadership in a Global Organisation:

Example 1:

Maya stopped by a restaurant after a few months of being away. The restaurant staff were excited to see her as she was a regular customer. They expressed their worry over her absence and wanted to know what had happened. Maya narrated how she had been fighting a health challenge which had prevented her from doing a whole lot of things. The staff were stunned by what she had gone through, and at the same time, could not hold back their joy that she was back on her feet again. One of the staff asked Maya if her health challenge affected her diet, and she said no. To celebrate her return to the restaurant, he served Maya her favourite meal and said it was on the house.

Maya must have felt special and loved. That level of personal attention and display of loving care must have swept her off her feet. The kind gesture displayed by the restaurant staff would probably lead to more referrals. The restaurant may have earned a customer advocate! Maya would probably make a social media post about it, tagging the restaurant, thus giving them more exposure.

That kind of personal attention did not start from Maya. It must have been practised among the employees of that organisation.

Henri J. M. Nouwen once said, "Hospitality primarily means the creation of a free space where a stranger can

In Conversation with Chris Nassetta (2020). 9:56-10:08. Retrieved from https://www.youtube.com/watch?v=NG6tELYjR14

enter and become a friend instead of an enemy. Hospitality is not to change people, but to offer them a space where the change can take place". This resonates with my perspective about hospitality as the act of being kind and giving a warm reception to guests or strangers. It is not about judging who is good or bad but about accepting people for who they are and being caring, loving, and respectful towards them.

Example 2:

Mike, a new employee at a car shop, received a call which made him agitated. A few co-workers saw his countenance and questioned him. At first, Mike hesitated, but he eventually told them that his daughter was involved in an accident and it calls for his immediate attention.

Mike was bothered because he was only a few days on the job, and he felt the situation would affect his job. While thinking of a way to deal with the situation, one of his colleagues, Jason, persuaded him to go take care of the situation. Others supported Jason and told Mike that they were ready to stand in for him.

On arriving at the hospital, Mike saw that the accident was ghastly and his daughter needed to undergo immediate surgery. He knew he could not comfortably pay for the surgery, and this got him worried.

A few hours later, his co-workers called to inquire about the situation and the condition of his daughter. Mike narrated what the doctor had told him and gave them the hospital's address, but left out his inability to afford the bills. Later that evening, his colleagues and his manager came visiting at the hospital. By morning, as a team of nurses wheeled Mike's daughter out of the Emergency Room, he tried to stop them, but he was told the bills had been paid and she was due for the surgery that morning.

Mike later realised that his co-workers had shared his daughter's medical bill amongst themselves. He could not contain his joy.

Mike certainly will not forget this kind gesture. He would never have imagined that his co-workers would go to such lengths for him, considering he was a new employee. This only confirms that the organisation where Mike works uphold love, care and unity as important virtues.

As a new member of staff, Mike's co-workers knew nothing of his character, but they stood by him and helped him as much as they could because they worked in a place where every staff mattered; whatever bothered one, bothered all. They were certain that the Manager would understand Mike's predicament and not hold it against him as long as he could get a medical report explaining the situation.

This kind of hospitality would keep the growth of any business without a reasonable doubt.

However, we must not overlook the fact that hospitality should not be expressed only by the host but also by the guests. Visitors and guests should not act entitled to hospitable gestures but should understand that they ought to reciprocate the love they get or wish to get.

Although some people may not return the respect accorded them, it is necessary to exercise patience, remain courteous, and welcoming. This may sometimes come as a challenge, but if hospitality is about accepting people as they are, then patience must be adopted in dealing with all men. More so, there is the possibility of influencing others with your care and kindness so much that they, in turn, start to also display these hospitable gestures. Hospitality is not just about the qualities of a customer but also their needs and wants, and how management adapts to them.

Hospitality has indeed existed since the beginning of man because it carries the principles of values that each of us possesses. It has played an essential role in our social life and careers. Today, hospitality is represented in all aspects of our lives, and although it does not allow for a specific definition, it still keeps to its original values of unconditional love.

17

KINDNESS AND CIVILITY

Hospitality is an act of kindness that elicits a profound positive moment of magic in the emotional bank account of the guest, visitor or stranger.
— Michael Idakwo

Profile: Michael Idakwo holds an MSc in Tourism, Leisure and Hospitality Management from the University of Science, Commerce and Business Administration, Benin; a PGD in Advanced Management Practice from Paris Graduate School of Management, France; and a Higher National Diploma in Hotel and Catering Management from the Federal Polytechnic, Idah, Kogi State.

He is a Fellow of the Institute of Management Consultants and Institute of Management Specialists, a certified International Professional Manager, UK; an associate member of the International Professional Managers Association, UK; and a Certified Management Consultant.

He has worked with Sheraton Hotel and Towers, Le Meridien Hotel, and Bolingo Hotel, all in Abuja, Nigeria, where he grew from the rank and file to the top echelon of hotel management. He is a Starwood-certified trainer, having been trained both in Nigeria and abroad. He is the Chief Executive Officer of Michel Hospitality Citadel, a hospitality consulting firm registered with the Corporate Affairs Commission.

Michael has been in the Hotel and Catering Industry for over 25 years and presently works at the Nisa Wellness Retreat, Abuja, as a hospitality manager. Michael invented a mocktail called Zomic delight while working with Le Meridien Hotel in 2005. He also authored a book titled *The ABC of Customer Service* in 2009, the first of its kind in this part of the world.

WHAT HOSPITALITY, ACCORDING TO MICHAEL, MEANS TO ME

The term hospitality is also derived from the word 'hospitalis' or 'hospitalitas' in Latin, which means 'hospitable' or 'hospitality'. The old French term was 'hospitalite', which means 'hospitable'.

Hospitality can be described as the generous and friendly treatment of visitors or guests. The opposite of being hospitable is incivility, which is a daily challenge faced by many in recent times.

Christine Pearson, a professor of global leadership at Thunderbird School of Global Management believes that uncivil and inhospitable actions, no matter how little, will have a high negative impact on performance, with a possibility of boosting aggression and violence in a person. This is particularly true because the emotional bank of every person is constantly affected by the gestures and reactions they get, and if they do not properly safeguard their sanity, there is room for corruption.

Years of experience have taught me that kindness must be constantly initiated because everyone has emotional needs that require fulfilment. Hospitality, according to Michael, is an act of kindness and generosity that elicits profound positive moments of magic in the emotional bank account of a guest, stranger or customer. Infusing kindness into every interaction will make relationships stronger, radiate the right expression, and retain returning customers.

In the long run, inhospitality is bound to bring nothing but ill luck to a relationship or business, which is why we must constantly reiterate the need for kindness and care towards every person we meet. Inhospitality can be seen even in simple acts such as looking away when you feel uninterested in a topic or presentation or texting during a meeting. The list could go on and on.

Inhospitality is not necessarily displayed out of malice or hatred but often from being inconsiderate or lacking forethought. It can lead to hate for some, and breed malice among staff. Every environment will always influence the behaviour of the people in it, and Christine Porath agrees with this concept. In a Ted Talk, titled 'Why Being Respectful to Your Co-Workers Is Good for Business', she stated that incivility is a bug and it is contagious.

Example:

There are, surprisingly, loads of stories of guests, strangers, and employees being treated inhumanely. Below are a few life examples. While you are reading these stories, be sure to note how some 'insignificant acts' could demoralise another person.

The manager who demeaned an intern[7]

When I was an intern at a PR firm, my manager would make me run her errands (pick up dry cleaning, ship things, drive her and her friends to SXSW events, etc). She would get my attention by calling me 'Intern' every time. At more than one off-site team-building event where alcohol was served, she not only pressured me to drink but made fun of me when I didn't give in. She also told me at length about her recent sexual exploits with a married real estate agent. Needless to say, when they asked me to stay on full-time, I politely declined.

---

[7] Stacey Lastoe. 'The Worst Boss I Ever Had: 11 True Stories That'll Make You Cringe' (2021). Retrieved from https://www.themuse.com/advice/the-worst-boss-i-ever-had-11-true-stories-thatll-make-you-cringe

The boss who blatantly disrespected an employee

I once had a boss who nearly always multi-tasked in meetings by being on her phone and present in meetings. In both one-on-one and group settings, she would shift her attention constantly from the speaker to her phone, back and forth, for the entire time. At first, I thought she was extremely busy, and it was the only way for her to get everything done, until one day. I caught her playing crossword puzzles on her phone while doing a check-in with me.

The boss who mocked an employee

At my first job, my manager was new to the game too and overbearing (i.e., she did things herself rather than empower her employees). We sat at a star-shaped table, so I noticed that every time I looked up, I made awkward eye contact with her. Initially, I liked the micromanagement since I had no clue how to do my job. After finally working up the confidence to lead a call, I remember trying to lighten the mood by saying a joke to the client. I watched as my manager (in my direct line of sight) immediately made a painful, over-dramatic cringe in response. My stomach dropped, and so did my excitement for the role.

These examples show the different ways kindness or inhospitality can affect a person's performance and emotional bank account.

In an article, 'The Price of Incivility'[8] published in *Harvard Business Review and Research*, professionals on incivility showed the negative effect of inhospitality on people, businesses, growth, productivity and self-esteem. The study showed that incivility has been recognised to be wrong, but many people fail to see its level of significance on people and businesses.

A poll was carried out involving 800 bosses from 17 industries to obtain the reactions of people who have been on the receiving end of incivility. The results from the poll can be seen below:

Value (%)	Reactions of people who experienced incivility
48%	Intentionally decreased their work effort.
47%	Intentionally decreased the time spent at work.
38%	Intentionally decreased the quality of their work.
80%	Lost work time worrying about the incident.
63%	Lost work time avoiding the offender.
66%	Decline in performance

---

[8] Christine Porath and Christine Pearson. 'The Price of Incivility' (2013). Retrieved from https://hbr.org/2013/01/the-price-of-incivility

78%	Commitment to the organization declined
12%	Left their job because of the uncivil treatment.
25%	Admitted to taking their frustration out on customers.

The results of the poll show the significant effect of inhospitality on performance and business. There is bound to be wastage, more expenses, and low performance. Incivility makes it hard to keep up at work; it pollutes the atmosphere, making the environment toxic and inconducive for productive work. The earlier CEOs, managers and everyone within or outside the hospitality industry understand this concept, the earlier its benefits can be properly harnessed.

A good look at the above statistics shows that small acts such as a smile, a congratulatory message, yelling at a guilty co-worker or a 'keep up the good work' message from a co-worker can raise or break the company.

18

EMPATHY AND CARE

Hospitality is showing empathy and care to every guest; it goes beyond reciting the lines in the company's SOP.
— **Brian Efa**

Profile: Brian Efa is the first indigenous General Manager of Ibom Hotel and Golf Resort. He is one of the rising stars in the hospitality and tourism industry and one of the very few Nigerians who have risen to this level in the industry. He is the Founder/President of the Nigerian Hotel and Tourism Investment Conference.

Brian holds a certificate in Finance Management from Hotelschool The Hague (Netherlands) and a certificate in Hotel Management from Wavecrest College of Hospitality. He holds a BSc in Accounting from the University of Calabar. He has attended numerous trainings in Nigeria and abroad including Harvard Business School, Lagos Business School, and John Maxwell Leadership Academy.

As General Manager of Ibom Hotel and Golf Resort, he has revitalised the resort within six months and made a great return on investment to its owners. The once-forgotten hospitality masterpiece is back on the tourism horizon. Before becoming a general manager, he spent several years in the finance department of the hospitality industry, including serving as Director of Finance, at Ibom Hotel; the pioneer Assistant Financial Controller, at Southern Sun, Ikoyi; pioneer Deputy Chief Accountant, at Le Meridien Ibom Hotel and Golf Resort, and Finance/Admin Manager, Le Chateau Hotel and Suite, Calabar.

In 2018, Brian was listed among the top 30 hospitality influencers in Nigeria and was recently inducted into the Top 100 Tourism Personalities Club for his contribution to tourism development in Nigeria.

The Harvard-trained finance expert has more than 15 years of experience in the industry. As managing partner of Jonel Hospitality Consulting, a hospitality investment advisory firm, Brian spent more than 6 years consulting for individuals, firms, and governments on the best approach to developing and investing in the industry to guarantee results. He has raised over $50 million of syndicate funds for hotel development in Nigeria.

WHAT HOSPITALITY, ACCORDING TO BRIAN, MEANS TO ME

Hospitality, to me, is not just reciting the lines in the Standard Operating Procedures (SOP) as handed over to the staff member by management. It is showing empathy and care to our guests.

The duty of any employee is not only to understand the procedures of the organisation but also to grow themselves in every quality that will make them and the company stand out. Hospitality involves interaction; it is not just a transaction. There must be a strategic yet empathetic flow of consistent communication between the organisation (staff member) and the guest.

Maddy Clark, Product and Technical Content Specialist at Hubspot, said, 'Sometimes, it can be tempting to get down to business right away, but remember to take the time to make things less transactional and turn tickets into more impactful interactions'.

How about periodically asking to find out how a guest is enjoying his stay in your hotel and offering to make his stay memorable? Don't you think this will bring them to a point where they can give honest feedback, knowing it would be heard and attended to without offence?

Asking about your guest's trip to your facility or even asking about their day could leave a lasting impression. What about randomly asking your employee how their day is going and if they need anything to work better? This is a great way to keep them in your constant embrace.

Everyone enjoys being cared for. Employees love knowing they can be themselves and still be allowed to get the job done.

So, you've served your customers and have made available all that you think they want. Yes, you have done your job, but is that all? Where is the exceptionality? What is the clear distinction between doing your job and winning your customers over?

Doing your job may not earn you a recurring client but being hospitable will. We must understand that we are in the infinite business world where the aim is to keep the business running and obsessed with satisfying the customers.

Hospitality is the thin line between serving your customers and winning them over. The key to bringing hospitality to life within an organisation is empathy.

There are three kinds of empathy: emotional, cognitive, and compassionate.

1.   **Emotional empathy:** It allows you to feel other people's emotions and distress; that is, you are moved by their situation so much that you absorb their distress.

2. **Cognitive empathy:** It helps you to understand the other person's situation and feel their distress but with a logical understanding of their emotions. It gives you an in-depth knowledge of what the person feels.

3.   **Compassionate empathy:** There is a difference between understanding a person's feelings and having the

desire to help. Empathy goes from feeling a person's emotions to understanding that feeling and eventually wanting to help. The desire to help a person in distress can be referred to as compassionate empathy. However, there is a need to stay aware even in our empathetic state because of its shortcomings.

SHORTCOMINGS OF EMPATHY

Empathy can sometimes be disadvantageous, and here is how.

In a situation where someone you are familiar with is against a stranger, there is a high possibility that you will be biased against the stranger. That is, our empathy tends to tilt towards our friends than strangers. Also, empathy as a response to other people's experiences can cloud our sense of judgment and right decision-making.

With the increasing talk about expressing love and care, there is still a prevalence of disdain where we decide for ourselves who deserves to be spoken to nicely. You may claim to be empathic, but it can only be justified by our relationship with people.

I remember the story of a psychologist, Tania Singer, who had taught so much about care and compassion. She preached a lot about empathy, describing the best ways to become a more empathetic being. These tips were relatable and practicable.

It was, however, shocking to read a report by *Science Magazine* in 2018[9], that Singer had been cruel to most (if not all) of her colleagues when she was Director at the Max Planck Society. She bullied, yelled and looked down on them, making it difficult for them to work with her, and treated pregnant women harshly. Colleagues who left expressed a feeling of relief.

She had the knowledge of empathy and care for others, but she did not use it; she let her perspective get in the way. Rigidity to perspective is a common reason for the many toxic behaviours people display.

Empathy is important to the employer, employee, and guests. To ensure your guests are treated rightly, be sure to create an environment that encourages hospitality. Simon Sinek said, 'As a manager or employee, you have to care for the people you're in charge of'. This encourages the love and care that your customer gets.

Hospitality, like everything else in life, requires balance and moderation. When next you are empathetic with that guest or employee, avoid being biased and maintain a clear sense of judgment.

---

[9] Kai Kupferschmidt. 'She's the World's Top Empathy Researcher. But Colleagues Say She Bullied and Intimidated Them' (2018). Retrieved from https://www.sciencemag.org/news/2018/08/she-s-world-s-top-empathy-researcher-colleagues-say-she-bullied-and-intimidated-them

19

LOVE AS A CUSTOMER RETENTION STRATEGY

Hospitality is loving people enough to create a memorable experience for them while serving and connecting with them.
— Ntewak Umoh

Profile: Ntewak Umoh is a hospitality business consultant, trainer, and hospitality service connoisseur. She holds a bachelor's degree in Banking and Finance and certifications in Hospitality Management, Hospitality Distribution, and Revenue Management. Her 11 years of experience within the hospitality industry have helped her hone her organisational, people-management, and leadership skills.

Ntewak is an ardent advocate for excellent customer service. She is the founder of Hotel Emergency Room, a hospitality business consulting company that helps hotels and food businesses with tools, resources, services, and intervention programmes that re-position them for growth. She has made an impact through various programmes such as the FBC workshop, a training programme that helps food businesses with their food inventory management, costing, and pricing; and Hospitality 360 Revamp, a signature programme designed to review, improve and sustain quality service in hotels and restaurants.

Ntewak is also a director on the board of Boardroom Apartments, an emerging lifestyle hotel apartment brand in Nigeria. She is committed to the growth and development of women in Africa and is a culture-diversity enthusiast. As an advocate for healthy eating, she creates healthy food recipes for families.

WHAT HOSPITALITY, ACCORDING TO NTEWAK, MEANS TO ME

Hospitality means creating a memorable experience for your customers through love and kindness while connecting with them. For it to become a lifestyle, it has to be deliberate. Many businesses adopt the 'customers are always right' mentality, not because they love them but because they want these customers to purchase from them irrespective of their flaws.

Simply loving the people you serve is the most basic but most important thing in the hospitality industry.

Josephine Ive supports that love for your clients is quite important in building a strong customer relationship. The basis of your relationship with your client should not just be the service you offer. It should extend to the emotional value you deliver and how it positively affects them, ensuring a balance when attending to customers individually.

If you love someone, there is a chance you want to create memorable moments with them. This should not be different when dealing with your customers; aim to treat them as you would a friend. This is a strategy that differentiates you from your competitors.

QUALITIES FOR HOSPITALITY

There is a need to ensure the heart is in the right place when exhibiting hospitality. What qualities do you need to be more deliberate about being loving and kind to your customers, irrespective of their facial expressions or utterances?

Here are some qualities that should be mastered to make hospitality seamless and attainable.

1. Patience is paramount if you must remain hospitable. Some customers will make you wonder if hospitality is essential. You could smile all you can and display all the expressions that should endear you to them, yet they still put up an attitude. The ability to overlook the reaction of that customer and keep being hospitable can be tasking but, once mastered, it can be a situation changer.

To lose patience is to lose the battle.
— Mahatma Gandhi

If you must win that customer over eventually, you must remain hospitable. Understand that some people may not be in their best mood; others may not be interested in being loved; while some are not used to it. Yet it shouldn't dissuade you from being hospitable. Whichever category your customer belongs to, remember Gandhi's quote and hold on to your patience.

2. Consistency is another crucial quality businesses should observe in all their dealings. You cannot be more hospitable to Mr X than Mr G; you should care for your customers equally and with top-notch service.

Consistency eliminates bias — which is a major problem in many organisations — as it keeps every customer at the top of the list. This is not to say that set levels based on service differentiation should be ignored. It means that the service package offered shouldn't determine the level of hospitality the customer receives.

Simply put, do not be more hospitable to a premium service customer and less to a basic or standard service customer. Consistency here portrays credibility and trust; it is a strong pillar on which relationships thrive.

3. Determination holds patience and consistency together. Relationship expert, Simon Sinek, constantly emphasises the need for patience and consistency in a relationship through determination. He affirms this in one of his notable quotes, 'Real love is delivered with genuine consistency'. Just like everything else, you must be deliberate in showing love because it is the determination that keeps you immersed in this love.

The constant display of love to 1, 2, 3, and 4 customers will boost the level of love you have to offer to customers.

Have you ever met an employee who felt irritated by her colleague's display of love for a customer? I have. As I fixed my eyes on this employee, I tried to observe why and how someone could be irritated by a sweet and beautiful gesture.

I was curious so I decided to be kind and loving to this employee. It was not easy, but I thought it was worth it, so I put in the effort. A few weeks later, I noticed that at his awareness of my presence in the building, this employee would look less stern. With time, he started making simple, caring gestures to employees and customers, which was touching for me.

This is proof that love and care can be taught and learnt when we put in the effort and are consistent with it. This also relates to how we respond to our customers. Not all of them will reciprocate or appreciate the love we show them; nevertheless, we must not let it affect our disposition. It should rather be a motivation and boost to our determination to do even more.

WHY HOSPITALITY IS IMPORTANT IN THE BUSINESS WORLD: CUSTOMER STRATEGY FOR BUSINESS GROWTH

Hospitality is a strong customer strategy for business growth. You need to genuinely love your customers to gain their trust and leverage their influence in the growth of your business.

To make relevant growth in your business with the help of your customers, you must understand customer strategy and its importance. In one of his videos, Brian Tracy talked about factors that back up hospitality as a business strategy. He said that when you focus on these three elements: customer retention, customer loyalty, and repeat sales, what you aim for will be achieved eventually.

Our aim is good financial standing for a business, but we must focus on the customers to achieve long-term wealth. This advice might sound stupid or inapplicable, but it is not. Every business that places a premium on hospitality for its customers records consistent and increasing business growth in the long run. The intentional work on the mastery of these factors recreates a productive, successful, and long-lasting business.

1. Customer Retention: Customer retention focuses on activities aimed at increasing the number of repeat buyers and maximising their lifetime value (LTV). It is more cost-effective to get repeat buyers than to look for new customers. While there's a certain appeal that comes with getting new customers, the ability to keep customers returning results in a greater ROI.

To achieve customer retention, you must provide support to your customers while offering help whenever and however necessary.

2. Customer Loyalty: Loyal customers are the most important tool in achieving business success. However, this has been debated, and over time, I have watched people spoil their customer relationships with broken trust.

Example:

Mathew has just located a company, XYZ, that makes his favourite footwear. He was excited about this, and before long, he became a loyal customer. As he continued to patronise them, he noticed a regular upward change in prices and asked the company about it. Rather than addressing the issue, they gave the excuse that the prices of some important materials have increased.

Despite his worry, Mathew continued to patronise XYZ but decided to contact three other companies that also make footwear. After much research, he gave one a trial and split the number of footwear to be made between XYZ and the new one. He received two quotes with a noticeable difference in prices but decides to patronise both companies two more times before making his final decision.

The new company's prices were cheaper than what XYZ has been selling to him, and both offer top-notch quality.

If it were you, what would you do?

Does this scenario remind you of that business you used to patronise? This is a common trend, where customer loyalty is not appreciated and importance is placed on profitability.

Some ways to ensure customer loyalty include sending a personalised email or following up on the preferences and information they might have shared during a discussion with you. Sometimes, such information may not be related to the services you render; but asking about it displays your thoughtfulness and attention to detail.

Through oral advertising, loyal customers bring more customers and drive referral traffic to your business.

3. Repeat Sales: Repeat sales are purchases customers make to replace a previously used product or service. The best way to make it in the business world is through repeat sales, which builds up your brand and brings better feedback. This is achievable through loyal customers. Brian Tracy says, 'Your company's most valuable asset is how it is known to its customers'. This means that your company does not make itself; it is the customers who make the company, and they are the greatest asset you will have in your business.

A continuous show of care and love reassures your customer that you have their best interest at heart. This serves as a constant reminder of how valuable they are to you and your business, which in turn gives them a reason to remain loyal even in their subconsciousness.

20
THOUGHTFULNESS

Anyone involved in the act of looking after or taking care of another can be said to be in the hospitality business.
— Wasiu Babalola

Profile: Wasiu Babalola is an associate professor in the Hotel Management and Tourism department, at Atiba University, Oyo, Nigeria. He is an adjunct faculty member/lecturer in the Hospitality Management, Tourism and Hospitality Unit at Lead City University, Ibadan, Nigeria. His teaching interest is currently centred on postgraduate studies in hospitality, tourism and marketing programmes.

Apart from academic roles, Dr Babalola is involved in several hospitality consultancy programmes. He is a member of the International Management Council of Continent Worldwide Hotels, Turkey. His work contributes to policy/decision-making and socioeconomic and manpower development of the hospitality and tourism industry.

He currently sits on the International Branch Committee of the Institute of Hospitality (IoH), UK–Nigeria International Branch as its honourary Chairman after serving as its honourary Vice Chairman and Chairman, CPD, from 2014 to 2017. He is also a council member of the Nigerian Hotel and Catering Institute (NHCI) and the Certified Board of Administration of Nigeria (CBAN). He is an alumnus of Lagos State Polytechnic with a PhD each in Hospitality Management and Forensic Accounting and Audit, and other qualifications in Catering and Hotel Management, Management, Human Resources Management, Marketing, Corporate Strategic Management and French - among others.

Wasiu is an author, educationist, and practising professional, holding fellowships of at least seven different professional bodies/associations in Management, Consulting, Hospitality, Tourism, Marketing, and Forensic Accounting, among others. His main research areas are hospitality operations, innovations & marketing, hospitality regulations, hospitality and tourism accounting, and forensics & sustainable development & planning.

WHAT HOSPITALITY, ACCORDING TO PROF. WASIU, MEANS TO ME

The hospitality industry encompasses businesses involved in providing comfort, leisure, food, drinks, and above all, caring for others. It consists of hotels, fast food, motels, restaurants, hostels, cafes, hospitals, old people's homes, prisons, etc. It also covers industrial and institutional catering, the hospitality consultancy business, tour, and travel operations, among others. These businesses offer services that help customers enjoy their free moments and make them feel good. The focus of the industry is the satisfaction of the customer.

As time passed, hospitality progressed from being an industry into being an act in most industries, but this has often been argued by many businesses that misvalue hospitality. Businesses in the engineering and manufacturing industry may undervalue it since they only exchange money for service.

Should it be so?

An excellent business should offer top-notch quality, comfort, and, most importantly, high-level hospitality to its customers. Their customers may not be at a spa or a hotel, but they love to be assured that they are in the right place, where value is placed not on their money alone but on them as individuals.

The hospitality industry has come to include what is now known as the aviation and transportation industry. Regardless, anyone involved in the act of looking after or taking care of another is said to be in the hospitality business; in which case, one can classify a housewife as part of the industry. It is in the embrace of a mother that you understand the essence of hospitality. Her acts are not driven by profitability but by the maximisation of available resources in satisfying numerous household needs. A mother's love exudes gracious care, one that is simple but thoughtful. This is the kind of hospitality that businesses need to show to amplify the effectiveness of their customer retention strategy.

Example[10]

Here is a real-life example of how much people can be valued and its possible effect on an organisation.

A couple, John and Gina, checked into Rendezvous Hotel one weekend to celebrate Gina's birthday. They had previously filled out a form on the hotel's website, and in its comment section, John had indicated the purpose of their intended stay at the hotel.

When they got to the hotel, they were welcomed warmly. The lady at the check-in counter, Sally, was very courteous and apologetic when she delayed the couple for about 4 minutes while trying to confirm their reservation.

Shortly after, the Guest Relations Manager showed them to their room, wishing Gina a happy birthday in the process. It didn't stop there. The couple was excited and surprised that

---

[10] Review of Rendezvous Hotel, Singapore. Retrieved from https://www.tripadvisor.com/ShowUserReviews-g294265-d299606-r360798278 - Rendezvous_Hotel_Singapore_by_Far_East_Hospitality-Singapore.html

the hotel staff had noted their comment in the online form and prepared something before their arrival.

The couple ended their review by saying, 'We are indeed thankful to the staff at Rendezvous Hotel for their thoughtful gesture, and we certainly look forward to more staycations there soon!'

As the saying goes, 'It's the little things...'

Some other hotel or organisation's staff may wonder what business they have with the birthday celebration or, at the most, propose a special birthday package for sale to the couple. Whenever our customers choose to do business with us, our responsibility is to make it worth their while.

Indeed, it is the little things that make the difference. Yes, it is the thoughtful gestures that separate you from your competition.

TECHNIQUES TO ENHANCE THOUGHTFULNESS

Hospitality is being thoughtful in situations, whether with strangers or friends. As basic as it may seem, it can transform a guest's experience.

Thoughtfulness is the key to customer retention. Thoughtfulness is the key to employee recruitment and satisfaction. Thoughtfulness is the key to brand perception. ... Thoughtfulness is free.
— Tom Peters

Here are some ways to improve your thoughtfulness:

1. Care for your customer: The true heart of hospitality is the value you attach to each person and not their spending power. To create an experience that would remain in your customers' minds, you should think about situations from their perspective, that is, how you can make things better for them. Ask yourself, what more can I do? If I take away the service they paid for, what will be left? Then think of a service you can offer that was not paid for, something they can hold on to when your services wear off.

2. Be aware of your customer: Notice your customer, pay attention to them, listen and observe. Find out what they value. You cannot be thoughtful when your mind is wandering or distracted.

3. Be willing to feel what they feel: Your customers are right in front of you, but do you see how they want to be treated? To be thoughtful in any situation, ponder on how you would love to be treated. An already angry customer wants to feel in control, a young couple wants to feel safe and relaxed, and a child, just like an adult, wants to feel pampered.

Hospitality is an industry and yet a lifestyle that sits at the core of any business. It embodies the value of serving and receiving. As a business owner, you are presented with daily opportunities to positively affect your customers and employees through thoughtful gestures while gaining their trust and loyalty.

If you take time to see from your customer or employee's view, you will find the little things that do not sit well and the thoughtful gestures that will fix the situation.

CONCLUSION

Different hospitality experts have spoken and given their opinions about the best ways to show hospitality. I am sure their insights have been impactful and have revealed how you can contribute better to the hospitality industry. In the end, the goal is to make a difference in the lives of the people you serve.

Hospitality can mean various things to different people, but one thing remains constant: making your guests feel good. How you express this rests on your understanding of your role in their lives.

The now-defunct Bank PHB made an advert where they showed that cars would drive themselves someday. In the advert, the car and its owner were engaged in a short discussion about the state of the economy. Their conversation went like this:

Car: I see all your shares are down. Are you thinking of selling?

Owner: Oh! I am buying big time.

Car: Wise move, Sir!

The car validated its owner's decision, leaving him smiling and a lot more relaxed than he had been when he first got into it. If the art of hospitality can be woven into the artificial intelligence of a car, it points to the many possibilities that exist when we begin to be more deliberate in how we serve. It also points to the obvious fact that we have to embrace and encourage hospitality within our teams.

One of the aims of every business is to remain sustainable; however, that is nearly impossible without a hospitable workplace, team, and culture. Businesses from all industries require hospitality to remain sustainable.

Through the adoption of hospitality, most businesses have experienced sustainability and relevance to their customers. According to a travel report in 2019, 70% of world tourists said they were more likely to revisit places that were friendly and more welcoming, irrespective of the location. That's the advantage of a hospitable system. Hospitality can give businesses an edge over their counterparts. It can lead to an increase in sales, productivity, quality, and customer loyalty, and improve brand image and reputation.

At the same time, a culture held together by hospitality will help businesses to harness the power of Corporate Social Responsibility (CSR), and the continuous development of CSR strategies will help organisations attain high-level sustainability.

Shelton Group,[11] in a study, discovered that 55% of US workers would prefer to work in organisations that are

---

[11] Tracy Stottler. 'The Importance of Sustainability in the Hospitality Industry'(2018). https://www.danacommunications.com/importance-of-sustainability-in-the-hospitality-industry/

socially responsible even if their income was a little less, while 77% would be more loyal to organisations that help them contribute to social and environmental issues.

Companies that consider the needs of their customers are more likely to have more loyal customers, which will lead to repeat sales. This is not to rule out the importance of profit, but you must find a way to tell your customers that they are loved and have a special place in the heart of your business.

Example:

Mr Joshua was an importer who had many importation offers. Teresa, his transporter, loved working with him because he never stressed her and was proactive in payments. His swift response, among other attributes, was exceptional. Teresa, on her part, was also sharp with her duties, getting only the best trucks for movements, actively monitoring his goods, and ensuring they were correctly delivered. She did more than was expected of her, especially in Mr Joshua's absence, promptly resolving monetary and regulatory issues.

They both enjoyed their business relationship because aside from delivering high-standard services, they were both exceptional in their dealings. Joshua would ask Teresa how work was going and if she was facing any challenges outside his job. Teresa would check up on him and help him get things done even in her absence.

One year into their business relationship, Joshua began to have difficulties with his business. He lost money and traders and went broke. Teresa found out when jobs stopped coming in regularly. She reached out to him, and based on the relationship they had built, he opened up to her. Teresa felt sorry for his predicament. She reduced her profit margin so that he could also make something tangible. She sent him funds sometimes. They met up to talk at work occasionally. She prayed for him and recommended him for jobs whenever the opportunity arose.

Joshua's wife gave birth around this period, and he invited Teresa to the naming ceremony. His wife was happy to meet her because of the good reports she had heard. Teresa was there with her son, who was overwhelmed by Joshua's hospitality.

While writing this book, I heard Teresa talking to her daughter about a customer who wanted to import goods. She planned to call Joshua immediately after the customer confirmed the details of the transaction.

This is what hospitality does: it keeps you in the good books of people, clients or workers. It makes you and your business approachable to everyone without fear.

According to Delery and Shaw (2001), collective human resource practices are important strategies that are capable of driving a company's sustainability. Many human resource personnel agree this is a fact. The customers are not the only ones entitled to respectable treatment; your employees are, too. How you treat your employees is a great way to know how best your customers would be treated.

As much as employers seek self-motivated workers, employees perform best when their efforts are supported with motivation from Human Resources (HR) practices. These practices include building hospitality acts such as friendliness, open communication, warm reception, and personal development activities like in-house training. Hospitality is naturally an integral part of HR, and the scale-up of an employee's performance can be linked to their commitment to the firm. HR practices would help boost how employees effectively carry out their duties, creating room for communication among other employees, customers and managers, which enhances overall organisational commitment and brilliant performance.

I have explored the experiences of various experts in the industry and can say hospitality goes beyond the industry or the paid services offered. It is a selfless act that when properly mastered, becomes a strategic management technique.

Adopting a culture of hospitality will increase your business's advantage, which will lead to staff and customer loyalty. Consciously imbibe a culture of hospitality in your business and watch the benefits accrue.